Anonymous

Investigation Into the Plans and Practices of Co-Operative Insurance Organizations,

chiefly those known as endowment associations

Anonymous

Investigation Into the Plans and Practices of Co-Operative Insurance Organizations,
chiefly those known as endowment associations

ISBN/EAN: 9783337219741

Printed in Europe, USA, Canada, Australia, Japan

Cover: Foto ©Suzi / pixelio.de

More available books at **www.hansebooks.com**

HOW THE ENDOWMENTS FIGURE.

Unsound financial schemes, like some of the so called "national" building and loan associations, and most of the proprietary endowment organizations, have the happy knack of so involving their victims in an inextricable maze of figures, denoting dollars and cents, that they are unable to grasp the situation. Like the uninitiated struggling with the "fifteen" puzzle, they, after repeated efforts to disentangle the problem, give it up in despair.

The Secretary of the Pacific Endowment League, instead of giving a plain, unvarnished exhibit of the financial operations and conditions of the league in his annual report, gives one of those interesting puzzles, going to show how the organization can fulfill its contract with the holders of coupons for the next two years.

There is not in said report a word or a figure showing what has been done with the large amount of money contributed by the members for the same expense fund.

EXPENSE FUND OF THE PACIFIC.

This league will not commence the levying of assessments until January 1, 1890, but from the day of its organization it has collected admission fees and quarterly dues, which go to the expense account. Let us see how much has been collected under these two items. It costs members $5 admission fee, and $1 50 per quarter for dues. Consequently the five thousand two hundred and eighty members must have paid in $26,400 admission fees. As each one must pay the first quarterly dues in advance, one quarter's dues, or $7,920, must be added to the former amount, making a total of $34,320.

The league has been in existence one and one half years, or six quarters, and as one quarter has been reckoned, we must strike an average as to the amount paid in for the remaining five. Take half the present membership, or two thousand six hundred and forty, paying five quarters, at $1 50, and we get $19,800. Adding this to the former figures, we get a grand approximate total paid into the expense fund of the league of $54,120. Where is the published statement, which should be in the hands of every member of the league, showing what has been done with every dollar of this amount?

All the genuine, well-conducted fraternal insurance associations publish periodical statements, setting forth the receipts and disbursements in every fund down to the last cent. All moneys are paid out by a warrant on the Treasurer, and the date, number, amount, and purpose of each warrant is clearly set forth.

From what has come to my knowledge, I find that most of the proprietary endowment institutions keep their expense account under lock and key. In the annual report of the Secretary of the Pacific League is the following:

We, the undersigned Finance Committee, have made a careful examination of the books of the Secretary and Treasurer for the fiscal year 1888-89, and have found them correct in every particular.

J. MARTINS, Chairman.
J. H. STRUCKMEYER.
JAMES McALLISTER.

Following this is the sworn testimony as to the correctness of the accounts by an expert accountant. This is all, no doubt, very satisfactory

INVESTIGATION

INTO THE

PLANS AND PRACTICES

OF

CO-OPERATIVE INSURANCE ORGANIZATIONS,

CHIEFLY THOSE KNOWN AS

ENDOWMENT ASSOCIATIONS,

BY THE

STATE BUREAU OF LABOR STATISTICS.

———

JOHN J. TOBIN, COMMISSIONER.

SACRAMENTO:

STATE OFFICE, : : : : J. D. YOUNG, SUPT. STATE PRINTING.

1889.

REPORT.

In the course of an investigation by this bureau into the extent and character of provident coöperation in this State, valuable information was obtained relative to the system pursued and the work accomplished in this direction by trades unions, fraternal societies, and coöperative insurance associations.

From the developments which arose regarding the plans and practices of the coöperative insurance associations, during the investigation, I have deemed it advisable to make a separate report of them, but especially of those called "endowment" associations.

All the information obtained relating to the provident coöperative features of the trades unions and fraternal societies will be published in the next biennial report of the bureau.

COÖPERATIVE INSURANCE.

Coöperative insurance in its various forms—life, accident, endowment, etc.—has come into existence within the last twenty-five years. Consequently it is yet almost too young to be judged as a permanent factor in our social economy, but its evolution is a curious and interesting study. It was begotten on the ruin and havoc wrought by the innumerable failures of life insurance companies. We are living in a progressive age; the "schoolmaster is abroad," and his lessons are bearing fruit.

When people saw high officials of insurance companies reveling in luxury and massing great fortunes from the money which they had contributed, they asked themselves the question, "Why should we not insure ourselves? If the officers and Directors of life insurance companies are able to hoard up millions of a reserve fund out of the payments of the insured, why should we not have a voice in deciding what disposition should be made of such funds? Through coöperation people of small means are able to conduct a business enterprise by uniting their little capital, which no one of them could possibly do alone, therefore let us coöperate."

The whole scheme of coöperative insurance is a strike against the sordid, selfish aggrandizement of old line insurance companies. Wage earners, men and women, wanted insurance to be paid in frequent small payments, but the agents who are interested in large premiums, and consequently large commissions, would not work such plans. By this course they killed the hen that laid for them the golden egg, because the people took the remedy into their own hands. Since the advent of the coöperative methods but few life insurance companies, on the old lines, have been incorporated where the former are in operation.

The new departure is most plausible in theory and commends itself to all who carefully study its features. In the hands of capable and honorable men it can accomplish a world of good.

The plan is simply for a number of people to combine in an organization; to charge for admission and annual or quarterly or monthly fees a sum sufficient for reasonable expenses; and to assess the member a certain sum, to be paid at certain periods, out of which is disbursed the amount of insurance to the member's legatee or beneficiary.

Such a plan to furnish money relief to an humble family at the lowest cost, and at time of great need—either in old age, or in case of accident or death—appeals to the masses as most deserving of support.

At first this plan was adopted by fraternal societies organized for other and different purposes, who put it in, so to speak, as a new plank in their platform. Those interested in the old line life and accident insurance companies tried, by every means, to cry down this new departure on the part of the fraternal societies. The country was deluged with literature showing the impossibility of success. Experts were employed who proved, beyond the possibility of contradiction, the utter absurdity of the fraternals being able to fulfill their obligations. "Figures don't lie," "You cannot go beyond the logic of cold facts," they continually cried out. Still, in spite of such direful prophecies and predictions, in the face of adverse arithmetical demonstrations, against all powerful monopoly influence, these fraternal societies have calmly pursued the even tenor of their way and faithfully carried out their pledges.

It may now be said that they have passed the experimental stage and entered upon a career of permanent usefulness. No one is now rash enough to dispute that the fraternal coöperative insurance societies have furnished an immense amount of relief at low cost.

METHODS OF OLD LINE INSURANCE.

They occupy a field inaccessible to the methods of the old life companies. They have forced the latter to a considerable reduction of rates, and brought them to a realizing sense that their days of undivided sway are passed forever. The enormous amount of money locked up in the reserve funds of the old line insurance companies, mounting up to the tens and hundreds of millions, is not now accumulating at such an alarming ratio. Take, for instance, the millions hoarded up annually and placed in reserve funds by the Mutual Life of New York, the Equitable Life Assurance, the Connecticut Mutual Life, and the New York life insurance companies. Where do they come from? They represent an amount over and above the necessary expenditures which was taken directly from the pockets of their policy holders in premiums. That it is proper for such companies to have a reserve or guarantee fund is unquestionable, even if the law did not require it, but to go on forever squeezing their shareholders in order to pile up this reserve fund mountain high, is baneful policy and unjust to those who pay. The thousands of insured who have raised up these immense piles from a cipher foundation have practically about as much present and prospective interest in the reserve funds, except in the way of guaranty, as the slaves under King Rameses had in the Egyptian pyramids which they had helped to build.

The Pennsylvania insurance reports show that the level premium insurance companies collected in ten years $699,250,701. They paid in losses and matured endowments during the same period $285,354,004. Where did the difference go, amounting to the enormous total of $413,896,797?

Twenty-nine companies in the State of New York received in premiums, in 1888, over $114,000,000, of which only $48,000,000 were paid for death claims, while $29,000,000 were paid for expenses. For every dollar, therefore, paid for death claims more than sixty cents was paid for expenses. The balance, $37,000,000, were added to the assets of the companies.

Consequently for every dollar paid for death losses about eighty cents was added to the already loaded and inflated reserve resources of these gigantic corporations.

No wonder that insurance magnates have been able to live in a style of splendor rivaling that of a Hindoo Maharajah.

The line at which the bleeding process must stop has been discovered by the coöperative insurance associations. On the other hand, so many bogus or fraudulent mutual or coöperative insurance companies have been organized, especially in San Francisco, that a provident head of a family may prefer to be bled by an old established company than run the risk of losing all in a mutual concern of whose character and ability to carry out its contract he has some misgivings. After the old fraternal societies (which merely extended their lines of usefulness) came new associations, lodges, guilds, etc., whose chief aim and object was professedly the insurance or endowment of their members, such as the Ancient Order of United Workmen, Knights of Honor, etc. Last, there followed stock or proprietary associations that commenced to work the assessment plan of life and endowment insurance as a business enterprise.

THREE CLASSES OF COÖPERATIVE INSURANCE.

We have then three classes of assessment insurance organizations:
1. Fraternal, with insurance superadded.
2. Assessment insurance guilds or lodges.
3. Assessment insurance associations.

Of the three classes referred to, the first, or strictly fraternal societies, such as the Ancient Order of United Workmen, Knights of Honor, etc., are looked upon as little republics, making their own rules and regulations by common consent, and therefore requiring no legal restraint or State supervision to protect the membership from imposition. I shall not refer to them further in this report, as full statistics concerning their plans and work will be given in the next biennial report of the bureau. It will be shown therein the vast amount of good being accomplished by such societies, especially in the United States and Great Britian.

Some of the second class are also conducted as genuine coöperative associations, honestly conducted, all the members pulling together in the same boat and sharing the same fortunes—sink or swim. Some again are sham fraternal guilds under the control and guidance of needy adventurers, who foist themselves into official position and manage to keep themselves there so long as the society lasts.

With regard to the third class, they embrace three forms of insurance organizations:
1. Insurance payable at death.
2. Insurance payable on account of sickness or accident.
3. Insurance payable during life at certain periods.

In this report I propose to deal only incidentally with the first two classes. As a general rule it will be found that, although ostensibly coöperative, they are in reality corporate or proprietary in their management. In the form of application for membership a clause is generally inserted by which the applicant gives his proxy or right to vote to the Directors of the association in the event that he is not present to vote.

In the case of one of these associations the applicant is asked to give his right to one individual Director named. As all the members are supposed to sign this form of application, the result is that they shift the burden from themselves and place the management in the hands of the

Directors, who are enabled by a continuation of the same methods of getting proxies to perpetuate their term of office. If this perpetuation of power should fall into the hands of good men, it insures the stability and success of the enterprise; otherwise, the usual train of folly, extravagance, and disaster follows.

THE HOME BENEFIT OF SAN FRANCISCO.

The Home Benefit Life Association of San Francisco is an excellent type of the mutual or assessment plan of life insurance. It was established in 1880, and reorganized in 1885, and from small beginnings has now reached a position where success is assured. Its growth has been steady healthy. The number of members is two thousand five hundred three; and the total income from assessments last year amount $135,335 85.

One third of the sum received from assessments is placed in the fund, which now amounts to $31,000. It belongs to the member returned to them at certain fixed intervals. Here lies one of points of difference between the old line company methods and mutual or coöperative. In the former a large proportion of the p paid by the insured went to swell the reserve fund. In the latte funds are not allowed to reach large proportions, but are regu tributed among all the members entitled to a share.

The plan of the Home Benefit in this regard is to place all the joining in any one year in the same series, like the plan of bui loan associations. One third of the assessments paid by each members is placed to his credit in the reserve fund of that ye At the end of five years all that has been paid into the reserv each of the members of that series is paid back to him, with tions from interest and lapses. He can get this amount in ca it to be used in the reduction of future assessments.

Consequently the reserve fund mainly consists of the one ments of members for five years. Not one dollar can be ta fund for expenses or other purposes.

The only condition under which it can be touched is for plication to the mortuary or death benefit fund, if a death of the normal should occur; and this is a wise precaut principle of such associations should be the prompt losses. The amount so taken, however, mus fund as soon as collected. This periodic with its profits, enables the persistent men fund towards reducing his insurance as he entitled to such a distribution or divide strong inducement to the insured to c feit what they had already paid in.

Another excellent feature in the H ment. The expenses of managemen was fourteen per cent of the total rec

When I entered upon this investig placed every facility at my disposa affairs. All the books and papers of tion. I was thus enabled to corrobor in to this bureau by the Secretary.

ENDOWMENT ASSOCIATIONS.

Again, in the third class are included the so called mutual endowment
ssociations, under company or proprietary management. They are, as a
general rule, unsound or bubble schemes. After a careful examination
f the plans of the endowments, and after procuring as much information
.s possible about their methods of doing business, I determined to hold
.n open investigation, in order to make as public as possible the nefarious
ractices of some of these associations. The testimony taken and received,
which is herewith submitted, is very instructive, and gives practical illus-
rations of the ways and means by which thousands have been deluded
.nd robbed.

California has become a hotbed for financial schemers, whose business
t is first to entrap and then to fleece unwary and unsuspecting dupes.
Some of the knowing, but over confident, ones are also frequently caught.
A great many of these schemes, under the mask or cloak of being mutual
.r coöperative, have been set afloat within the past few years, and the cry
s "still they come."

San Francisco has the misfortune of being the headquarters or base of
perations, from whence the agents of these schemes are sent all over the
ountry to prey upon the gullible. As a natural consequence, San Fran-
isco is supposed to nourish and back these new-fangled schemes, which
.re masquerading under the popular ægis of coöperation. It is time to
e up and doing, that the fair name of the metropolis of the State may
lot be smirched and become a word of reproach to thousands of victims
eyond our borders. In most of the Eastern States laws are in force which
hut out such impostures. There is an imperative necessity for similar
rotection in California, as will be shown by the facts set forth in this
eport.

About thirty thousand members are enrolled in the endowment associa-
ions of California. The principal associations in San Francisco and Oak-
and have a membership, in round numbers, as follows:

Jnited Endowment Associates	5,500
.egion of the West	2,500
toyal Argosy	2,000
'acific Endowment	5,000
iuaranty Endowment	2,000
Cureka Endowment	1,500
.futual of Oakland	1,000
;quity Benefit	500
Total	20,000

This leaves a balance of ten thousand for the small associations in San
Francisco and other cities of the State. There are about fifteen thousand
nembers in addition belonging to life, sickness, and accident insurance
ssociations, on the mutual or assessment plan, that claim to be exempt
rom the supervision of the Insurance Commissioner and not to come
within the purview of our insurance laws.

As the usual admission fee is $5, the thirty thousand members of the
ndowments must have paid about $150,000 for the privilege of having
heir names placed on the roll. This goes to the general or expense fund.
There is a quarterly charge besides for expenses of management, which
isually amounts to $6 per year for each member, making a total of $180,-
)00 per annum.

Taking the average monthly rate of assessment for the endowment or
nsurance fund at $2 50, or $30 per year, nearly $1,000,000 per annum would

be drawn from the members for that fund alone if they were all levying such assessments. Fortunately they are not. Several at present are content with raking in the coin which is paid for admission fees and quarterly dues, and is sacred to the uses of the management.

From the large number of persons interested in these endowment associations and on account of the heavy interests involved, the necessity and expediency of a report concerning their status and methods can at once be seen, especially in view of the fact that they are not required by law to publish such a report themselves and are not under the supervision of any State authority. Ostensibly all of these organizations are coöperative insurance associations, formed for the mutual benefit of the members and not for profit.

It will be found upon reading this report that many of them are only sham coöperatives, and that they have been organized for the profit of a few inside managers, who have everything to gain and nothing to lose by the success or failure of the enterprise. Most of them are based upon glittering and specious plans, alluring to the unsophisticated, who are drawn into them by the thousands. To such an extent has this craze gone that now no miracle of converting tens into thousands is too astounding, and no scheme of acquiring capital in two or three years by means of small monthly installments is too extravagant or impracticable in the eyes of the gullible public. All that the plotters, who float these schemes, have to do is to see that their lines are well baited with seductive promises and shoals of gudgeons will rise to the surface and bite. As a natural consequence endowment associations of this class are as thick as blackberries, and the number of their victims is legion.

While the contracts made by these associations are in form and substance life insurance policies, it borders on the ridiculous to designate their methods as of the same business character as those of the regular life insurance companies.

The articles of incorporation in themselves are without objection, as they set forth the coöperative benevolent objects of the organization. It is in the execution of the plan—the carrying out of these benevolent objects—that the organization deserves either censure or condemnation. In the prospectus and other publications we find the scheme of these associations outlined. The endowment associations issue a certificate of membership, which is an agreement to pay to the insured, at stated intervals, of from one to ten years, a certain sum specified. The extent of the interval generally depends upon the age of the member upon entering—the greater the age the shorter the interval. They also, in most instances, issue a beneficiary certificate, which is simply a contract to pay to the heirs of the member or his nominee in the policy a stated amount at death. The consideration for both agreements is assessments to be levied upon the members of the association. The amount of each assessment is fixed by classification, or regulated according to the age of the insured in tables, so that a member generally knows the amount of his assessment, but as the levying of them is left to the judgment of the Directors he cannot tell the number he has to meet during the year.

NO PROTECTION UNDER THE LAW.

Unfortunately, in California there is no government protection from barefaced imposition and misrepresentation on the part of wily, designing schemers, who organize these fraudulent endowment, accident, and life insurance associations under the pretense of benevolent or fraternal coöp-

9

eration. The State Insurance Commissioner is powerless in the matter, because Section 451 of the Civil Code of California takes them from under his supervision. It reads as follows:

SEC. 451. All associations or secret orders, and other benevolent or fraternal coöperative societies, incorporated or organized for the purpose of mutual protection and the relief of its members, and for the payment of stipulated sums of money to its members, or to the families of deceased members, and not for profit, are declared not to be insurance companies in the sense and meaning of the insurance laws of this State, and are exempt from the provisions of all existing laws of this State.

This section was enacted to enable mutual or coöperative insurance organizations to do business in California, and also to relieve genuine fraternal organizations, such as those referred to in the first class, from any annoying interference from non-members with their secret internal affairs. The old line insurance companies fought the bill through every stage unsuccessfully. The object of the law was good, but it was perverted from its original purposes, and used as a shield or barrier to protect schemers in their nefarious transactions from official overhauling.

In their literature most of the bubble schemes parade the fact that they have been incorporated under the laws of the State of California. This is done for the purpose of creating the impression that they are subject to State inspection, or obliged to send in reports at stated periods to some official, or that the State holds some of their securities for the protection of members. Some of them, however, never incorporated at all, and, so far as the interests of the membership are concerned, it is a matter of very little consequence, for incorporation does not protect.

Section 382 of the Civil Code of California provides that the Attorney-General or District Attorney, whenever, and as often as required by the Governor, must examine into the affairs and condition of any corporation in this State.

Outside of this conditional direction there is no provision of the law making it obligatory on any government officer to examine into the affairs and condition of such institutions. Consequently, the citizens of California can be duped and plucked and victimized at the sweet will and pleasure of every designing knave under cloak of land, building, loan, endowment, accident, patent, mining stock, and other schemes. Exposures in the public press from day to day do not drive these rascals from the ground. Suppressed to-day, they bob up serenely in some new disguise to-morrow.

ENDOWMENT TRANSFORMATIONS.

Like the Grand Llama of Thibet they never actually die. They are *metamorphosed*, or undergo simply a transmigration of soul. If knocked on the head as a " Pacific " institution, they reappear as an " Occidental;" and if deprived of breath as an " Equity," they come " in questionable shape " as a " Fidelity."

For instance, when the Pacific Coast branch of the "Mutual Self Endowment and Benevolent Association of America," with headquarters at Longview, Texas, departed this life, its soul transmigrated into the Pacific Mutual Self Endowment Association. Upon the decease of the latter it underwent a transfiguration and came up smiling as the Occidental Self Endowment Association. When the last went the way of all flesh, the faithful were told to worship at the shrine of the Western Mutual Benefit Association.

The following is a list of defunct endowment associations that first drew the breath of life—not an honest breath—in this State and suddenly gave up the ghost, leaving countless mourners behind. They sprung into existence full of the seeds of death, spluttered like a midge in the sunshine, and then vanished:

DEAD ENDOWMENTS.

Mutual Endowment Association of Los Angeles.
National Relief Association of San Francisco.
Young People's Insurance Society of San Francisco.
French Mutual Aid Society of Sacramento.
Occidental Mutual Endowment Association of San Francisco.
Pacific Mutual Aid Society of Los Angeles.
Union Endowment Association of San Francisco.
Southern California Mutual Aid Association.
San Francisco Safety Fund Association.
San Francisco Universal Benevolent Association.
Pacific Coast Provident Association of Sacramento.
Pacific Coast Branch of the Mutual Self Endowment and Benevolent Association of Texas.
Pacific Mutual Endowment Association of Oakland.
People's Life and Accident Association of San Francisco.
California Life and Endowment Association of San Francisco.
Youths' Mutual Endowment Association of San Francisco.
Minors' Mutual Endowment Association of Livermore.
Pacific Coast Mutual Endowment and Protective Association of Santa Rosa.
Order of Mutual Companies.
United Friends of the Pacific.
United Order of Honor.
Farmers' and Mechanics' Indemnity Association of Fresno.
Guardian Mutual Endowment Association of San Francisco.
Phœnix Fiduciary Endowment Association of San Francisco.
Tontine Society of Oakland.
California Benevolent Guild of San Francisco.
United Endowment League of San Francisco.
United States Mutual Benefit Association of San Francisco.

The schemers who stood by the cradle of these death inhaling abortions were not to be seen weeping over their coffin at the grave.

Long impunity in wickedness begets recklessness and disregard of public opinion. Some of the very men who have been publicly denounced by name in the press and from the platform as villains of the deepest dye and deserving of public execration, are still to be found prominent in associations whose objects are professedly those of fraternity and benevolence. Their finger marks can be found in the plans of several endowment associations now in full blast, and nothing but the strong arm of the law can save the public from their machinations.

HOW PEOPLE ARE FLEECED.

As an illustration of the bold and unscrupulous manner in which citizens are fleeced, the following article from the San Francisco "Chronicle," which has unceasingly exposed these impostures, is deserving attention:

TO BE WOUND UP.—INVESTIGATING THE UNION ENDOWMENT.—TWO THOMPSONS' TRICKS.—BOTH TO BE PROSECUTED.—MEETING OF SHORN POLICY HOLDERS.

The last of a series of meetings of the policy holders of the defunct Union Endowment and Mutual Benevolent Association of America was held in Odd Fellows' Hall yesterday afternoon. Dr. Newell called the meeting to order and mentioned its objects.
Mrs. L. C. Stratton, on behalf of the Investigation Committee, stated that an expert had been employed to go through the books, and that his report was ready.
J. D. Ford, the expert referred to, was then called upon to make public the results of his examination. The bank accounts, as shown by the ledger, the cash book, as shown by the vouchers, and the assessment and due books he pronounced correct as far as they go. The private accounts of the Directors show that James Alexander paid into the association $208, and drew out $272, while the books still show a credit balance of $176; O. C. Wheeler paid in $108, drew out $438; B. and Charles C. McDougall paid in $237, and drew out $337; Smith B. Thompson only paid in $346 and drew out $2,451, while his credit balance amounts to $424; his two sons, William H. and F. R. Thompson, paid in together the

munificent sum of $108, and drew out $3,330; so that the three Thompsons paid in $454 and received in return $5,781, or nearly $13 for $1. Continuing, the expert showed that in addition to the salaries of the Thompsons, amounting to $125 each, they received $10 for every meeting of the Directors, although such meetings were held in the offices at the Odd Fellows' building.

The vouchers for the furnishing of the offices cannot be found, and those who supplied the carpets, etc., state that they cannot find the account. The bonds of S. B. Thompson and of his son are not to be found. An item in the books charges $25 30 for the incorporation certificate of the State, whereas the actual cost was $15 30. The association is also charged $34 for books and blanks made out in the name of the Grand Union Mutual Life, Health, and Accident Association of the United States, with headquarters at Danville, Pennsylvania, though no reason is assigned for the charge. Only fifty of the blanks are to be found, and they bear the name of Smith B. Thompson as agent of the long named association.

The most weighty discoveries made, and those which created quite a sensation, were that the first ten pages of the assessment ledger and the first six pages of the dues register have been cut out. A note appears on the pages of the first book stating that the missing leaves were obliterated by the spilling of the ink and are to be found in the safe. Only one leaf was found, and it has the appearance of having had the ink rubbed into it. Five death claims were paid by the association according to the books, and the beneficiaries in three out of the five cases were the Thompson family. Smith B. Thompson's claim of $527 was paid in full, but the duplicate certificate has not been found, and the original policies of Sarah M. Case's claim, from Camden, New Jersey, are also missing. Egbert Thompson died in May, 1887, and Welcome A. Thompson in August, being, as one member put it, the "wrong Thompson to die." The balance on hand, as shown by W. H. Thompson's account, was $80 short of the amount entered on his balance sheet, amounting to $477.

TRICKS OF THE TRADE.

Another remarkable example of the methods employed by the schemers who set afloat these fraudulent endowment schemes is given in the following article taken from the same journal. It will be seen from this, as well as from the last article, that these schemers stop at no villainy to screen themselves from exposure and consequent punishment. Books and papers are mutilated or destroyed; receipts and vouchers are torn up; the absent and the dead are personated; widows, orphans, invalids, and aged persons are victimized and robbed:

THE OCCIDENTAL OFFICERS TO EXPLAIN.—NUMEROUS FRAUDS CHARGED.—HALF A MILLION TO BE ACCOUNTED FOR.—A NEW SCHEME FLOATED.

At last an attempt is to be made to check the unscrupulous methods of that class of endowment associations which has been repeatedly held up to public view in the columns of the "Chronicle." A suit was filed in Department 5 of the Superior Court yesterday by Carl Spelling, a Santa Rosa attorney, for his client, Adele Pieper, against the Occidental Endowment Association, as represented by W. E. Taylor, the City Coroner, Harr Wagner, J. L. Liddle, the President, George C. Jones, the Secretary, J. B. Church, J. D. Gray, A. W. Kelsey, C. S. Richman, and several others. The plaintiff asks for an accounting, and has filed a complaint which covers twenty-two pages of legal cap in typewriting. Her name appears in the case at the instance of a number of the members, all of whom are anxious to have the business of the association investigated, and to have the officers punished if found guilty of the crimes sworn to in the complaint.

The opening pages of the voluminous document trace the connection between the association sued and its predecessor, the bankrupt and defunct Pacific Coast branch of the Mutual Self-Endowment and Benevolent Association of America, the headquarters of which were in Longview, Texas. The connection with and identity of the officers of both the dead and the now insolvent society are pointed out with much minuteness, and the facts pertaining to the assumption by the Occidental of the Mutual's liabilities are historically presented, with a complete reprint of the constitution, by-laws, and contracts of the two associations.

Miss Pieper goes on to state that on January 3, 1884, she became a member of the "Texas swindle," as it has been called, and agreed to abide by its laws, paying the necessary fees and assessments for a $5,000 policy. In August, 1887, the Mutual ceased to do business. The lady changed over to the Occidental, according to the terms of the latter's offer, and continued her payments until January 3, 1889. At that date her first coupon of $1,000 became due and was not paid. All she has received has been $100 advanced to her at the rate of eight per cent per annum in January, 1885.

From this point the plaintiff makes the most damning allegations against the defendants. She charges that, with the other members, she has paid into the association sued $500,000, out of which the defendants have conspired together to defraud the members and creditors of the society. Eight separate counts are cited in support of the assertions.

These may be briefly summed up and are as follows: False and fraudulent entries have been made in the books; fraudulent reports have been made to the members regarding the receipts and disbursements of the moneys and the business affairs of the society. An inspection of the books has, it is said, been refused the members, and all knowledge of the true financial condition of the corporation has been suppressed. The defendants named are accused of having appropriated $100,000 of the funds of the corporation, and of having, through agents and personally, sometimes in the names of their agents and sometimes in their own names, bought up apparently past due coupons and paid them to themselves in full, in so doing making away with about $100,000 more. In the same way they are accused of having bought fictitious assignments of claims and of paying to themselves the claims in full, amounting in the aggregate to the sum of $100,000. The last count states that by other fraudulent means the officers paid to themselves on purchased certificates the sum of $200,000, and the names of alleged holders of eighteen certificates of $1,000 each, all paid in full, are cited in proof of the assertion.

The most interesting part of the document is comprised in the closing seven pages. It will be remembered that J. J. Vasconcellos sued the association last month for $1,757, and that the suit went by default, the Sheriff attaching the office furniture, books, etc. This suit, the plaintiff alleges, was purposely allowed to go unanswered in order that the defendants might bid in the books at public auction, and then destroy the evidence of their transactions.

The sale was advertised to take place yesterday morning at eleven o'clock, but the plaintiff's petition for an injunction of the Court restraining the Sheriff was served a few minutes before the sale was to have commenced, to the great consternation of the association's officers, who were present in numbers. Mr. Laumeister was ordered to deliver the books up only on the order of the Court.

The complaint closes by asking the Court to investigate the business of the corporation as conducted by its officers; that she be awarded $887, the balance due her, and that a receiver be appointed. Fox, Kellogg & King of this city are of counsel to Carl Spelling, Miss Pieper's attorney.

The effrontery of the officials of the concern is illustrated by the fact that T. J. Brooke, J. L. Riddle, and George C. Jones have issued circulars urging the members of the Occidental Endowment Association, which they admit has expired, to join a new concern, called the Western Benefit Union. The offices of this association are at room 10, Flood building, and C. E. Lesher and F. T. Morelle, late members of the Occidental, are sponsors for the fledgling. All who join are led to believe that they will get what the sued society owes them, although in another paragraph the liabilities of the latter are repudiated entirely. Both Lesher and Morelle were employed to buy in lapsed policies, and draw the amounts of matured coupons, for which the managers of the Occidental gave themselves credit, leaving a wide margin of profit.

WHO THE VICTIMS ARE.

Their victims can be found in almost every town in the State, for the agents of these vile schemes are ubiquitous and irrepressible. They spare neither age nor sex. The more innocent the victim, the more easy to be at first allured and then betrayed. An evidence of this can be found in the following dispatch to the "San Francisco Chronicle" from Santa Rosa:

THE ENDOWMENT SWINDLE.—WIDOWS AND NEEDY PEOPLE UNSCRUPULOUSLY FLEECED.

SANTA ROSA, April 22.—Widows and credulous persons seem to have been the principal objects of attack of the Occidental Self-Endowment Association. Widows were especially solicited to become members. To this end a woman was engaged in the business of soliciting lady members, and success crowned her efforts. One widow yesterday said to a "Chronicle" reporter: " I joined the association after being solicited to do so, and was assured that it was on a substantial basis. It was explained to me as a loan society. I drew my first loan, which was $100, without any trouble. When the next payment was due I was put off. I insisted on having my money, when I was informed, to my surprise, that the organization was not a loan society and was never intended to be. Of course I could do nothing. I had already paid quite a sum of money and could not afford to let my policy lapse if there was a chance to get back the money I had paid in. In a few weeks more I received notice that the assessments had been doubled.

" I sought advice from the Directors, who are Santa Rosa business men. Two informed me that they did not know anything about the concern, one ending his remarks with the words: ' When my assessments are due, I pay them.' The other said those organizing the company came to him and asked permission to use his name. Continuing he said: ' I found out that I could not become liable for anything, and told them to go ahead. I don't know much about the affairs of the association.'

" During the winter months," continued the lady, " I used to sew while in bed till late into the nights, that I might economize in my wood bill, so the assessments might be met. My coupon is due in July, and the company has failed. I have paid in about $350."

A janitress,of the public schools has paid a good many dollars from her small and much needed salary into the coffers of the association.

Another widow, who has a mortgage on her place, has been anxiously awaiting the maturity of her coupon that she might pay off part of her incumbrance.

CHARGES AGAINST THE ENDOWMENTS.

As the purposes and practices of these non-fraternal coöperative insurance organizations are strikingly similar, a diagnosis of a few will suffice for all. In what I have to say I expressly and emphatically disclaim making reflections upon the character or motives of individuals. Neither do I charge that they are dishonestly conducted, for I know comparatively little of what is done with the fees and dues that go into the expense and other funds. What I have to do with is the plan of the organization, and the way that plan is carried out. In other words, I have to do with the *ship* and its *course*, and not with the *crew* and *cargo*.

I do charge, however, that they afford wide scope for iniquitous practices, and the fact that rascals have availed themselves of the opportunity is evidenced by the large number of disastrous failures reported in the press, with all their rank-smelling disclosures. I also charge that, with very rare exceptions, they are mere money-making concerns, sailing under the false color of a benevolent or fraternal coöperative society; that their tendency is to enrich the few inside managers at the expense of the membership; that the methods of nearly all are unsound, and their promises delusive, and collapse will be the inevitable result.

These proprietary institutions, if attacked, try to shield themselves under the armor of genuine coöperative organizations which have established a good reputation and become deservedly popular. " Our plans," they will argue, " are similar, and why not work as well ? " " They promised more than we have promised, and have experienced no difficulty in performing as they promised, and were never in so flourishing a condition as to-day," said the President of one of them in an open letter addressed to the Labor Commissioner.

CONTRAST BETWEEN THE FRATERNAL AND PROPRIETARY.

There is a vast difference between a truly fraternal organization and one under the management of a few individuals, who are in it for selfish purposes. Although the latter deny that these institutions are organized for profit, no sensible person will believe that the officers are merely working for glory. The members in the fraternal associations are like men in a boat pulling together, who, in case of danger, will cast overboard all dead weight and incumbrances, who will work with a will as one man, and, in the hour of want and extremity, will divide their scant stock of provisions share and share alike. The members in the proprietary associations are like guests in a large hotel, who, in case of fire or danger, try to escape with what little they can lay their hands on, and rush out regardless of what happens to others. Some of them, judging from testimony given, are not over particular as to whether it is their own or their neighbors' property they carry off in the general scramble. "Every man for himself. and the devil take the hindmost," is the motto of these pseudo coöperatives.

When the drain upon their resources grows deeper and deeper, as maturing coupons increase, the fraternals, having a practical knowledge of the situation, vote for the continually increasing assessments because of the necessity, and because they know that all the members of the lodge have to do the same. But when a member in one of these proprietary endowments receives additional notices of assessments, and finds himself in the dark as to the reasons therefor, he soon throws up his membership in disgust.

PROPRIETARY ENDOWMENT PRACTICES.

From the evidence given before me by J. J. Vasconcellos, of San Francisco, it appears that one of the nefarious practices of the Directors of these proprietary endowment institutions is to go around among members holding policies nearly matured (but which had been forfeited by lapsing in the payment of assessments) and buying them up for a mere pittance. These policies had never been canceled on the books of the association, and even if they had they would be returned and the amount of the matured coupon cashed by the officer of the association who had bought up the certificate. Another nefarious practice, as shown up in evidence in Court in San Francisco, is for an inside organizer of one of these associations to procure an aged dummy member as representative, whose dues, etc., would be attended to by said "insider," in order that he may have the first coupon mature sooner than if it was in his own name. Several reliable persons have informed me that the practice of holding powers of attorney on behalf of dummy members is quite common. By this means it would be impossible to detect by an examination of the roll of membership who were really the persons who would be entitled to draw cash for the first coupons maturing. John Doe on the roll would be the dummy representative of a Pecksniffian Director who, for obvious reasons, wished to conceal his identity. On the other hand, some of the proprietary endowment associations are in the hands of men of respectable social and business relations who, even if they are in error as to the inevitable outcome of the enterprise, will not steal the funds nor countenance jobbery. Take, for example, the Mutual Endowment of Oakland, the officers of which are citizens of well known probity. Where, however, as among these associations, there is so much chaff—so much that is corrupt or open to suspicion—it is difficult to sift out the wheat. The managers of these companies, in their leaflets, make the point that the members are not required to attend lodge meetings, which means that the inconvenience and trouble of attending to the affairs of the association, weekly or monthly, are removed from the shoulders of the members and placed upon those of the half dozen or so individuals who constitute the Board of Directors. To call such endowment companies *coöperative* is a misnomer and a distortion of the term.

The gentlemen who beget the schemes not only elect themselves officers and Directors, but take the necessary steps that they shall be succeeded only by themselves. This is done by means of proxy votes. Only the managers are acquainted with the names and addresses of all the members. What so easy, then, when the day of annual election approaches, than for these officials to hold the necessary number of votes to reëlect themselves? Do we not see the same thing done every day by Directors in mining stock companies? Again, members scattered all over the State can take little or no active part in the affairs of such an institution. At the annual meeting members living at a distance, say from Shasta or San Bernardino, cannot attend without considerable loss of time and expense. The offices where such meetings are supposed to be held could accommodate only a very small fraction of the membership. The association will not defray their expenses or allow them a per diem.

15

15

THE LODGE SYSTEM.

Under the lodge system all this is done. The expenses and per diem of representatives of lodges from remote districts are paid by the association. A large and representative body of members come together to deliberate and transact business of common benefit to all. Such organizations deserve to be called *coöperative*. That there are no lodge meetings to attend, therefore, instead of being an inducement, should be a hindrance to a person becoming a member. Lodge meetings mean that the members have the management of affairs in their own hands. No lodge meetings mean that four or five members or individuals manage affairs to suit themselves. These so called associations are, then, practically private companies or corporations, without the corresponding risk of capital usual on the part of the Directors. The way the thing is done is about as follows:

HOW ENDOWMENT ASSOCIATIONS ARE ORGANIZED.

Four or five persons, with an eye to the main chance, get together in some back room and concoct an endowment insurance scheme, with some high sounding title like the " Fidelity Mutual Guarantee Self-Endowment Association of America." They draw up a set of by-laws, elect themselves officers and Directors; send the necessary papers and fees to the County Clerk and Secretary of State for incorporation, and they are ready to do business under the great seal of the State.

The only additional expenses required are the payment of office rent, a little in advance, and either the purchase or hire of a desk, chairs, etc. Some printing, showing forth the stupendous merits of the scheme, has to be done, which can be paid for as soon as the fees commence to flow in.

The schemers and plotters are now ready for business. Agents are employed to work upon the gullible, and rake in the coin for admission fees and quarterly dues.

WOMEN CANVASSERS.

Women are found to be excellent canvassers for endowment schemes, and, in consequence, are very generally employed to bring in others of the sex. Women are less disposed than men to study out the problem as to how one dollar can multiply itself into five in the course of three or four years. Eve did not enter into a mathematical or theological discussion with the Devil in the Garden of Eden. As many of them say, " They have no head for figures." It is enough for some of them to learn that " Mrs. or Miss so and so got $500 the other day when her coupon became due, and she had paid in less than $100." The deduction naturally follows that they also will receive the value of their coupons when due. They do not reflect that, like in lottery schemes, for the one prize there are a thousand blanks, and for the one woman who got her coupon cashed there are a thousand who found the concern bankrupt when their coupons fell due. One of the canvassers in petticoats succeeded not long ago in inveigling about a dozen poor factory girls into joining one of the rankest endowment associations in San Francisco. These canvassers receive from $1 to $3 of the initiation fee of each member they bring in, and when they are in the country they receive more for traveling expenses.

PLANS OF THE ENDOWMENTS.

The plans or objects of these institutions, although having a verisimilitude, are as dissimilar in detail as the patches of a "crazy" quilt. Each one starts out with "new features," immeasurably superior to all the other schemes in operation. The difference between the endowment system and the regular life insurance is that the former pays to the holder while living the face of the bond or certificate, while the *latter* pays to his legatee the face of the policy after death. The endowment or distinguishing feature of all these associations consists in a contract or agreement to pay a fixed sum, generally from $250 to $1,000, at certain stated periods of time. As a rule these periods are fixed at intervals regulated according to the age of the individual who becomes a member. In most of the associations the age of said member is deducted from seventy-five years and the result divided by the number of coupons attached to the certificate. For example, if a man upon entering was thirty-five years old and there were ten coupons of $500 each attached to his certificate of membership, as the difference between thirty-five and seventy-five years is forty he would be entitled to receive $500 at intervals of four years, the result of dividing the forty years by ten, the number of coupons.

Of course, as the interval of payments is the shorter the greater the age of the member, so also the amount of assessment to be levied in order to pay the coupons is increased according to age.

Some of these endowment schemes divide the intervals at which coupons are to be paid irrespective of the age of the member, and vary the assessment schedule accordingly.

For example, the intervals would be divided into three classes called A, B, C, the coupons being made payable at intervals, respectively, of five years in Class A, four years in Class B, and three years in Class C. The assessments to be paid in the last, or Class C, would of course be higher than in the others, and those to be paid in Class B higher than in Class A.

Many of these associations discard the death benefit entirely, so that in case of death the beneficiary named in the certificate of membership has to continue the payment of dues, assessments, etc., the same as the original holder, or forfeit all moneys previously paid in. Under such a plan why there should be an artificial regulation of intervals according to the age of a member when coupons become due and payable is somewhat perplexing. The boy of sixteen and the old man of seventy are on the same plane when, in case that death intervenes, the payment of assessments must be continued by the living legatee. It is simply done to give the plan an insurance air, by throwing a mysterious glamour in the form of a schedule of figures and tables by which the thing has been and can be solved.

The division of periods into classes of two, three, four, etc., as before mentioned, and assessing the members accordingly, is the intelligible method under such a scheme. Some pay the full amount of the next to mature coupon in case of death. Some pay only a small amount for funeral expenses, but no coupon or insurance.

Where there is no death benefit or insurance, no medical examination is required upon admission. This feature now seems to be most popular. The dislike to undergo such an examination, coupled with the desire to get hold of a lump sum, instead of leaving it to legatees, attracts the multitude. It is therefore not surprising that the endowment associations which have no policies to pay in case of death, and require not the services of a medical examiner, are the ones with by far the largest membership. Such a system may be considered mercenary and selfish. A member of an endowment association insures for himself, and not for his family. The helplessness of orphan children and the forlorn condition of the penniless widow are often forgotten in the carnal desire to "eat, drink, and be merry," and let the future take care of itself.

ASSESSMENTS AND DUES.

The certificate of membership contains the gross sum for which a person is insured, and the coupons attached the fractional part of said amount, obtained by dividing it by the number of coupons. If the certificate is for $5,000, and there are ten coupons, each coupon would be for $500; if eight coupons, $625, and so on. In some associations the number of coupons attached to certificates is the same to all members. In others the number is regulated according to age. For example, all who enter under forty-five years may be entitled to ten coupons, and after that age to eight, six, etc., as may be set forth in the by-laws.

Some of them increase the assessment upon the members as they advance in years, while others let it remain fixed as it was on the day when the member joined the association.

The amount of the entrance fee varies according to the amount for which a person insures, and runs from about $5 to $30. Quarterly dues are usually about 50 cents a month, but often exceed this amount. Transfer fees of from $1 to $3 are charged when a member transfers his stock to another or when he changes the name of his beneficiary. These fees and dues go to the expense fund. In many of the associations it is provided that any surplus remaining shall revert to the assessment fund for the benefit of the members.

In the short experience we have had of their practices, a *deficiency* instead of a *surplus* is usually seen in the expense funds. The proprietary endowment concerns do not, with one or two exceptions, publish detailed reports of their financial operations, especially as to what becomes of the fees and dues that go into the expense fund.

From the death-bed developments of the ephemeral endowments that "fretted their busy hour" in this State, it appears that the inside plotters and schemers not only gobbled all the cash of the expense fund, but every dollar for beneficiary or other purposes which they could lay their hands on when the crash came. With this class the scheme of mutual self-endowment is a game of self-enrichment.

NO PRINTED BY-LAWS.

Another most significant fact is that very few of these proprietary endowment concerns publish their by-laws. Both in the form of application and in the certificate of membership a member promises to obey the by-laws of the association, and no copy of these laws is placed in his hands. He therefore promises to comply with conditions and obey laws he knows nothing about. When asked for a copy of their by-laws, the answer is that they have not been printed because of the expense. Such was the answer given by the Secretary of the Guaranty Endowment Benevolent Association, which claims to have over two thousand members. In the face of the large amount received for admission fees (more than $10,000) and quarterly dues, the plea that the institution could not afford the small expense of printing their laws is very weak indeed. They could afford to spend a large amount in fitting up their offices, but not the few dollars required for printing. The so called coöperative association that will not print or distribute the laws which govern it, deserves to be placed in the suspicious class *ipso facto*.

When additions and alterations are made in the laws the members are not notified of the fact. In the open investigation the President of the Western Mutual, when asked "How can the members be informed of a

2-L

change in your by-laws when they are not printed?" was unable to answer. Who can tell anything about the plans and practices of these organizations under such circumstances without overhauling the books in their offices where such rules are written?

Why, its own members cannot tell how the laws of the organization can be or have been enacted, altered, or amended. They do not understand what power is vested in the five gentlemen who have the management in their hands—how or when they were, or are to be, elected, or what is their term of office.

SURREPTITIOUS CHANGING OF BY-LAWS.

In the testimony given before me by Mr. J. H. Leonard, City Treasurer of San José, it was shown that the Directors of the Western Mutual Benefit Association so changed the laws of the association that the terms of their contract with the membership were altered in order to deprive, if possible, a poor widow of her just claim against the Western Mutual.

If printed and distributed the members would be in a position to learn that these by-laws are often changed to suit the purposes of the officers. It has been the practice to have the by-laws so drawn at the time of organization that the periods of maturity of coupons shall be short and the assessments small, in order that the inside managers may be the first to cash coupons and entice others to become members. After a time the by-laws are amended and a new assessment and maturity table is formulated with higher assessments and longer periods of maturity, so that while a charter member can get his coupon cashed in from two to three years, a later member of the same age will have to wait a much longer time.

Authority to amend the by-laws generally rests with the officers, thus obviating the necessity of calling a meeting of the members. Officers are not obliged to give any notice of their intention to alter the laws and are not limited to any particular occasion, but may do so at any time. Their law-making power is as unrestricted as that of an eastern autocrat. If any inquisitive member, exercising his right under any existing law, should attempt, for instance, to examine the cash accounts he could be told to call again in a few hours, and, in the mean time, a private meeting of the officers might be held and an amendment to the by-laws, depriving the member of said right, could be adopted.

In looking over the prospectus of the Guaranty Endowment I noticed that the coupon maturity and assessments table was headed "Department B." Upon inquiry I found that the former maturity and assessment table, which was "Department A," had been withdrawn, and I could not procure a copy. Why it was withdrawn I could not discover.

The Mutual of Oakland, according to the Secretary, has about doubled its rates of assessments. About two hundred of the original members enjoy the privileges of the old tables, and are thus enabled to get their coupons cashed for far less money than those who entered later. All the members of the Mutual, according to the testimony of its Secretary, are duly notified of any change made in the by-laws.

The Eureka Endowment, which has about fifteen hundred members, increased the original rate of assessment about 20 per cent, and at the same time lengthened the "maturity table." For example, the assessment on a $5,000 certificate for a person of from thirty-five to forty years of age in the old table was $2 50. In the new it is $3 05. The coupon of a man fifty years of age matured, according to the old table, in two and one half years; in the new it will take three years and four months. The old people who were early in the field have, accordingly, much the advantage over the late arrivals.

WHY ASSESSMENTS ARE POSTPONED.

In some the levying of assessments for the benefit or endowment fund begins from the date of organization. In others it is deferred for from one and a half to two years, until they gather a large number into the fold. The fact that assessments will not be levied for a considerable period is a strong inducement to people to join, so that they may rank among the first to get their coupons cashed. Besides, it is a great satisfaction to be assured that the period of the maturity of your coupon is growing daily less, while you are not called upon to contribute a dollar towards its redemption. People do not stop to ask themselves where the money is to come from that will redeem these coupons. "Grapes do not grow upon thistles, nor figs upon thorns." It must be evident that where the increment of profit does not grow at the ordinary business rate, the increase must come from the pockets of victims. Somebody has to pay the piper, and each member lives on, pays on, in the hope that he is not to be among the unlucky ones. In the meantime fees and dues are pouring into the expense fund, which is sacred to the uses of the officers and Directors.

The Pacific, organized March 8, 1888, will not begin to levy assessments until January 1, 1890, or after a period of more than one year and nine months.

The Guaranty, incorporated July 19, 1888, will not do the same until June 1, 1890, or in one year and ten and one half months.

The Eureka, incorporated November 5, 1888, will not do the same until June 1, 1890, or in one year and seven months.

From the very date of organization they have entered into a contract with their members to pay them a certain amount in a certain time, and still allow a considerable portion of that time to elapse without demanding a dollar for investment as an increment of profit. Take an original member of the Eureka, for example, of fifty years of age, who takes out a certificate for $5,000. How much has he to pay, provided he becomes a member at the date of the organization, November 5, 1888? His first coupon for $500 will mature in two and one half years, that is, on May 5, 1891. He pays for admission fee $5; quarterly dues, at $6 per year, $15; and monthly assessments from June 1, 1890—that is twelve months—at $3 35 per month, which amount to $40 20, making a total in all of $60 20. For this he receives $500.

Happy pioneer of the Eureka Endowment, you can well cry "Eureka" when you pocket the twenty-five shining $20 gold pieces in exchange for the three you paid in. How is it with the man who comes later? The member of the same age who takes out a certificate of $5,000 on the first day of June, 1890, will not be so fortunate as the pioneer referred to. The fees and the dues will be the same—$20—but he will have to pay monthly assessments for three years and four months, at $4 20 per month, amounting to $168, making a total of $188.

He will have to pay, then, more than three times as much money and have to wait nearly a year longer than the pioneer Eurekan before he can march off with his $500. Hence it will be seen that the "early bird," in the endowments, is the one most likely to "catch the worm."

The early member in the Pacific and in the Guaranty enjoy still greater advantages over the one who comes in after the assessments begin, because they have a longer period of non-assessment than in the Eureka. An

original member of thirty-five years of age in the Pacific would have to
pay assessments for only two years and a quarter, when he would be
entitled to cash for his coupon, while the one of the sâme age who comes
in after January 1, 1890, must pay assessments for four years. The former
has to pay in assessments only $60 75 for his $500, while the latter has to
pay $108. What can be said of a business enterprise which admits of
such gross incongruities and palpable favoritism?

Take, for example, one thousand members of the Pacific, who had the
good fortune to join at an early date. They would have paid in $60,750,
and be entitled to draw out $500,000.

As the average rate of assessment amounts to $27 per year, it would
take a thousand members nearly twenty years to pay this sum, or five
thousand members, nearly four years. In all human probability before
this devoutly to be wished realization of the expectation of said one thousand pioneers, the Pacific will have gone the way of all endowments, leaving thousands of mourners behind, who had not come within hailing
distance of the promised coupon.

The Secretary of the Pacific, in his first annual report, states that one
hundred and twenty-four coupons of $500 each, amounting to $62,000, fall
due in the year 1890. As the average assessment per year is $27, the for-
tunate members who will pocket the $62,000 will have to pay in assess-
ments only $2,348, and will make a clear gain of $473 on an investment
of only $27.

In the following year coupons on four hundred and twenty-three certificates, amounting to $211,500, fall due. The happy owners of these certifi-
cates will have to pay in assessments from $27, beginning the year, up to
$54 at the end, or an average say of $45. They will have paid in, therefore, $19,035, and be entitled to draw out $211,500.

Prodigious profits! During the first two years of assessments—that is,
in the years 1890 and 1891—five hundred and forty-seven members, who
will pay in only $21,383, will draw from the treasury of the Pacific $273,-
500. The average amount paid is less than $40 for each member, for which
he is entitled to draw $500. Who are to be the fortunate drawers of the
prizes? Who will be the happy five hundred that will make this glorious
raid upon the treasury? It is to be presumed that the nine perpetual
Directors of the Pacific will look out, not only for their own individual
interests, but for that of their friends, during these two fruitful years. It
would indeed be interesting to know who are the one hundred and twenty-
four members entitled to draw $500 each during the last four months of
next year from the treasury of an association organized March 8, 1888.
The Secretary states that the average coupon maturity is four years and
one month, but these fortunate insiders will draw $62,000 long before the
Pacific reaches the age of three years.

GROUND PLAN OF ENDOWMENTS.

The following classification indicates to some extent the ground plan of
many of these schemes:

1. Certificate of membership, with coupons attached, payable at certain
intervals, but in case of death, the full face of the certificate is to be paid,
less amount of coupon, if any, previously cashed.

2. Same as No. 1, but only the next maturing coupons to be paid in the
event of death.

3. Same as No. 1, but nothing to be paid at death, except a small benefit
for funeral expenses.

21

4. Same as No. 1, but nothing at death. The beneficiary named in certificate can continue payments until next coupon matures.
5. Same as No. 1, with benefits, in case of sickness or accident, added.
6. All or a portion of the assessments paid back to members, under conditions, and at stated periods.

THE EQUITY BENEFIT.

One of these, known as the "Equity Benefit Association," charges for admission fees from $8 to $15, and for annual dues from $5 to $20. Ten per cent is taken off the receipts for assessments, which run from $2 50 to $10 per month, for a reserve fund. The plan of the "Equity" is as follows:

On the last day of each month the amount in the benefit fund shall be disbursed to the members in good standing in the following order: First, one tenth of certificate No. 1 shall be paid in full *if due by maturity*, otherwise the holder of the certificate shall be paid *double the amount* he or she has paid into the Association and be required to accept such amount in *full payment of one tenth* of certificate, and shall be furnished a new certificate for *one tenth less* than the original certificate, *bearing new number and date*, and maturing accordingly, the same as a new certificate. Then one tenth of certificate No. 2 shall be paid in the same manner, and so on, payments being made on the first part of each certificate to members in good standing in regular numerical order, until the amount in the benefit fund is *exhausted*, or until the balance left in the fund is not sufficient to pay the certificate *next due double* the amount received on that certificate. On the last day of the next month the first part due of certificate next to the one paid last shall be paid in accordance with the above plan, and each other certificate in regular numerical order, until the fund is again exhausted, and so on each succeeding month thereafter.

This is one of the associations having a reserve fund. Besides the very large membership fees and semi-annual dues which go to the expense fund, 10 per cent of the monthly assessments are also taken from the members and put into what is called a reserve fund.

In some of the best conducted fraternal organizations they have no reserve fund. Such funds, though essential in a well managed insurance company, are a standing temptation to fiduciary officers in the endowments, and the establishment of them is a return to the old insurance methods, which coöperatives rebelled against. In the bursted concerns no trace of any coin in the reserve fund could ever be discovered. It was *reserved* for the managers.

The "Equity Benefit" has about six hundred members. Although incorporated since February 5, 1886, no laws governing it have been printed. The members are therefore groping in the dark coöperatively. Any person of ordinary intelligence can see at a glance that the scheme is designed to put money in the purse of the few who first become members, and therefore have the lowest numbered certificates. The advantage of this plan over others is that the managers, or the insiders, have not to wait very long for their share of the profits, as they are divided monthly.

THE FIDELITY.

The Fidelity Endowment is somewhat upon the same plan as the Equity, and under its "first series," or original plan, considerately promised its members double the amount they had subscribed. Finding that it could not stand the strain upon its resources, it wisely reduced the amount to 50 per cent upon the investment. The double payment plan would work as follows:

Suppose twenty members organize, at the end of the first month the first ten on the roll would pocket double the amount they had paid in, or the whole proceeds paid in by the twenty. At the end of the next month the receipts of forty members would be required to pay the second ten double what they had paid in. To pay the next twenty double what they had paid in would require eighty new members, and so on increasing at a ratio which would quickly reach the millions. In the meantime the members who originally doubled their money would be paying assessments for those that followed, without any hope that it would ever come to their turn again.

Experience has shown that they are not such fools. Some of the pioneers, having pocketed 100 per cent on their investment, quietly stood from under, and departed.

THE NATIONAL.

Another, called the "National Endowment Association," promises to pay at the end of each year $200 for a monthly assessment of $5; that is, to disburse $200 for $60 received. No limit to the number of shares! This is such an outrageous and barefaced scheme to perform impossibilities, that it is almost incredible that any one, except a person demented, could take stock in it.

From all that I can learn, it is a corporation sole. A single individual is "polyofficered," like the Grand High Executioner in the Mikado, and is President, Secretary, Treasurer, and Finance Committee rolled into one.

Ten per cent of this scheme also goes to the reserve fund, so that actually the National promises to pay $200 for $54 in a single year. For a time the names of the officers of this concern were printed in the prospectus, but in consequence of exposure in the press the names are now omitted altogether. A letter of inquiry about it from Michigan was referred to me by the Mayor of San Francisco, which shows that agents are employed to take in gudgeons in other States.

THE EAGLE.

"The Eagle Insurance Society" offers to insure any one, young or old, for as many thousand dollars as they may see fit to pay for. No medical examination required.

In this society the following plan of mutual endowment insurance is exploited: Any person, male or female, old or young, may apply for membership, and, if accepted, become a member on paying an entrance fee of $10 and $5 for each subsequent $1,000, with monthly dues of $1 25, of which $1 shall go to the reserve fund. The benefits claimed for this system are that for each $1,000 paid into the reserve fund the member in good standing holding the lowest number of membership in the society shall be entitled to $1,000. Should a member die before his or her endowment becomes due, and be at the time of death in good standing, the amount paid by him or her will be refunded to the legal representatives of the deceased.

In the application it is set forth that the member "shall be subject to the rules and regulations of the constitution and by-laws of this association, as they now read, and any new section which may be hereafter added, and all the alterations and amendments which may be made and adopted from time to time."

As a sort of a spur to the energies of the society, the following sentence is printed on the back of the circular: "Our members are requested to dis-·tribute these circulars; we want to run our membership to a million."

Let us take the statement in the circular of the Eagle Insurance Society that they want a million members, and assume, for purposes of illustration, that they have one million members. With one million persons paying $10 initiation expenses the promoters of the society secure at the outset a nest egg of $10,000,000, and as this membership of one million will pay during the first year $3,000,000 for running expenses, at 25 cents per capita a month, and $12,000,000 into the surplus fund at the rate of $1 per capita per month, we will have at the year's end, according to the circular of the company, only $12,000,000 to draw from, as there is nothing in the application securing the $10 initiation fee as a fund available to the members.

We will say in the first year of the existence of the Eagle Insurance Society twelve thousand members receive $1,000 each of the total of the reserve fund of $12,000,000. That will leave nothing on hand for the remaining membership of nine hundred and eighty-eight thousand persons, who all expect to receive $1,000 each, or a total of $988,000,000.

Of course in the absence of medical examinations, and the uniform rate for the infant and the octogenarian, the death ratio will be frightfully increased, as compared with the experience of long established insurance companies, and there must be a constant army of recruits coming in to keep up the payments; but as to this payment question it will be seen, by reference to the application blank of the company, that its provisions and responsibilities are subject to alteration and future amendments.

Suppose a man dies, the society will give him back the money he had paid into the surplus fund; that is to say, $1 per month; but it, of course, does not return the additional 25 cents per month, which goes into the expense account of the society. He has virtually been paying 25 per cent interest to the society to take care of his money for him.

THE YOUNG PEOPLE'S.

The Young People's Insurance Society is another of the same character, in San Francisco, only substituting $100 for the $1,000 certificates.

They are far worse than a lottery scheme, for in the latter, if honestly conducted, all stand upon the same plane and have an equal chance of drawing a prize, but in the former the prizes fall to the few on the inside who hold the lowest numbered certificates.

THE PACIFIC ENDOWMENT LEAGUE.

"The Pacific Endowment League" was organized March 8, 1888. The management is in the hands of nine Directors.

These gentlemen formulated what is called a "Code of Laws," which is so ingeniously drawn as to confer perpetual and almost absolute control in their own hands.

Article I of this code provides: There shall be a Board of nine Directors, invested with full power and authority to enact laws for the government of the league, and who shall choose from among their number a President, a Vice-President, a Secretary, and a Treasurer.

Although the organization boasts of having more than five thousand members, these nine members, who constitute the directory, have alone the power to enact laws binding upon all. Nowhere else in this remarkable "code" does it state how these laws can be altered or amended. Is this coöperation? Is this giving each and every member an equal voice in the framing of laws governing the whole?

No time or place is set in the code when or where the laws can be so enacted by these nine Directors. They can do so at their own sweet will and pleasure.

As the Pacific Endowment League has never been incorporated as an organization for coöperative purposes, it is difficult to understand what the league is composed of, except a league formed for purely private business purposes by the nine gentlemen who compose the directory. If all the members constitute the league, why should not the organization be made a legal body by incorporation? How can the rights of the individual members be guarded and protected in any Court of law under such circumstances? In whose name can suits be entered or defended? What recourse has an aggrieved member against the organization? As it is not an incorporated body, then who adopted this code of laws, and by whom can they be altered or amended? There is no provision in this remarkable code of laws for the election of officers at stated periods.

THE PACIFIC A SHAM COÖPERATIVE.

As there is no term of office specified, the gentlemen elected may be considered permanent or life-term officers, who can play battledore and shuttlecock with the "code of laws." They have full power to fill all vacancies. The code provides that an annual meeting of the members shall be held at San Francisco on the first Tuesday of May, 1890, and on the first Tuesday of May of every year. At such meetings *two thirds of the entire membership* shall constitute a quorum for the transaction of business. Suppose they had seven thousand five hundred members on their roll next May, there must be at least five thousand members—two thirds of seven thousand five hundred—on hand at the meeting before any business could be transacted. Even if the membership did not exceed six thousand, the officers would have to rent the Mechanics' Pavilion in San Francisco, for their meeting, to accommodate the four thousand members who constitute a quorum. There is no provision in the by-laws for voting by proxy. Members would have to flock in from remote States and Territories to attend this annual meeting, and for what purpose? To elect three Directors—nothing more. "The mountains have labored, and a miserable mouse is brought forth." It is a transparent humbug for these four thousand members to come together and not have a voice in the alteration or amendment of their code of laws or in the election of a President, Vice-President, etc. The remaining six Directors would still hold the fort, having the power to remove the three so elected upon charges preferred. But, it may be argued, such things cannot be done under the Civil Code of California, which safely guards and protects the rights of the members. Yes, if it is an incorporated organization. But the Pacific Endowment League of San Francisco is not, and the members are at the mercy, pleasure, and good will of the nine gentlemen who constitute the directory. How can the members of such an organization have any rights or privileges not expressly given and held in leash by the nine gentlemen composing the directory? It must be concluded, therefore, that the coöperative features of the scheme are a mockery and a delusion.

THE BANKERS' MUTUAL RELIEF.

The Bankers' Mutual Relief of San Francisco, in the laws governing the association, says its " object is to bind together in mutual interests for assistance in case of sickness, accident, and death, and to promote a feeling of friendship and union of action in benevolent work."

The fraternal and coöperative features of the association are exemplified in this, that the officers of the association, who, of course, are the originators of the scheme, hold office for one year, or *until their successors are elected.* As there is no provision in these laws as to when or where the annual meeting of the members will be held, there is not much danger of the Directors being disturbed. The laws of the association "may be amended at any time by a majority vote of the officers."

In the form of application for membership is the following: "I declare that a majority of the Directors of this association shall have power, in my absence, at any and all future meetings of the members of this association, to act as my attorney in fact and deposit the vote to which I would be entitled."

THE FIDELITY MUTUAL AID.

The Fidelity Mutual Aid Association, also organized in San Francisco, is precisely similar in its aims and objects to the Bankers' Mutual Relief. In the prospectus is the following: "By associating together acceptable persons they become entitled, by a common bond interest, in mutually aiding each other during sickness, accident, and death, and each, contributing his mite, succeeds in lifting the burden from the other's shoulders." What beautiful, consoling, and truly fraternal language. How edifying the idea of one brother "lifting the burden from the other's shoulders." The true state of the case is that the members know as much of each other and of what is being done in the "lifting" line as they do of the man in the moon and the internal affairs of that satellite. As the by-laws are not printed, the members are ignorant of what they are.

In the form of application of the Fidelity Mutual Aid, the same as in the Bankers', the applicant gives his power of attorney to the Directors to vote for him at all meetings of the association. This is "lifting the burden" of taking part in the management of the association from the shoulders of the members and placing it on those of the self-sacrificing gentlemen who constitute the directory. No printed reports from officers showing what had been done with the moneys paid by the members have been distributed.

THE EUREKA.

In the laws governing the Eureka Endowment Association of nearly two thousand members, the Board of Directors of seven members are endowed with absolute power. They can "enact and enforce all such laws as they may at any time deem for the best interests and welfare of the association." It is significant that at annual meetings of the members, according to Article XVI of said laws, it takes two thirds of those present to alter or amend these laws, which four of these self-constituted Directors have in their power to do. Remarkable from a coöperative point of view! This Board of Directors choose from among themselves a President, Vice-President, Secretary, and Treasurer, and the President appoints a Finance Committee, so as to give office to the remaining three Directors. They have full power to levy as many assessments as they deem necessary. They can reject any applicant for membership.

Like in the Pacific, it requires two thirds of the entire membership to constitute a quorum for the transaction of business at the annual meeting. As the probabilities of this proportion ever coming together are about as remote as in the case of the Pacific, before commented upon, the Directors of the Eureka may rest consoled that they shall never be disturbed in their mutual coöperative benevolent undertaking.

In the same way it will be found upon examining into the coöperative features of all these non-fraternal organizations (which parade the fact that their members have no lodge meetings to attend) that the management is vested in a Board of from five to nine Directors, who are practically irremovable. Either in the laws framed by themselves, or in the form of application, or in the certificate of membership, there is inserted some clause which will give them practically, though not nominally, an unlimited lease of arbitrary power.

THE MUTUAL OF OAKLAND.

In the certificate of membership of the Mutual Endowment Association of Oakland occurs the following:

A majority of the Board of Trustees shall have power, in the absence of the member herein named, at any meeting of the association, and in the absence of any proxy of said member, to represent and deposit the vote or votes to which said member shall be entitled.

According to this, at the annual meeting for the election of officers, a majority of the Directors can cast the vote of all the absent members who have not sent in proxies. What a simple, guileless method of perpetuating their own term of office. As the number of absentees at such annual meetings far outnumber those present and voting, the officers are not in much danger of being ousted. The Mutual Endowment Association of Oakland, although more than five years in existence, has never published a statement of the receipts and disbursements of its general or expense fund. As it not only charges high rates of admission fees, but also expropriates 10 per cent of the monthly assessments for this fund, the amount received must be very large. In most or nearly all of the endowment associations the monthly assessments are placed, without any deduction, to the credit of the endowment fund; but the Mutual is not satisfied with the usual sources of income for expenses, and takes 10 per cent of the assessments. Have not the members a right to know what becomes of their admission fees of from $10 to $30; of their dues from $3 to $30 paid every year; and of *one tenth* of their monthly assessments? What are the salaries paid to officers, and how much is paid for other expenses?

The financial statement of the Mutual of Oakland for the half year to July 1, 1889, is similar in style and character to that issued by an insurance company, and does not give such full details of receipts and disbursements as would be expected from a coöperative undertaking. As in the case of the Pacific of San Francisco, it may be intelligible and satisfactory to the half dozen gentlemen constituting the directory, but certainly not to the body of the members. For the said half year $6,115, out of a total of $39,000, that is, about 16 per cent, is transferred to the reserve fund, which already amounts to $50,000. As this reserve fund expands year after year it will represent an accumulation taken from the members and put in the hands of perpetual Directors. Experience has shown, in the case of old line insurance companies, that this leads to extravagance, high salaries, etc., and often to investment or speculation for the benefit of those in charge.

From a company or corporation point of view, the Mutual of Oakland may be a worthy institution and deserving of confidence. What I object to is its pretense of being a coöperative or mutual association, when its methods are proprietary and similar to insurance companies that comply with the laws relating to insurance and are under the supervision of the Insurance Commissioner.

HOW THE ENDOWMENTS FIGURE.

Unsound financial schemes, like some of the so called "national" building and loan associations, and most of the proprietary endowment organizations, have the happy knack of so involving their victims in an inextricable maze of figures, denoting dollars and cents, that they are unable to grasp the situation. Like the uninitiated struggling with the "fifteen" puzzle, they, after repeated efforts to disentangle the problem, give it up in despair.

The Secretary of the Pacific Endowment League, instead of giving a plain, unvarnished exhibit of the financial operations and conditions of the league in his annual report, gives one of those interesting puzzles, going to show how the organization can fulfill its contract with the holders of coupons for the next two years.

There is not in said report a word or a figure showing what has been done with the large amount of money contributed by the members for the same expense fund.

EXPENSE FUND OF THE PACIFIC.

This league will not commence the levying of assessments until January 1, 1890, but from the day of its organization it has collected admission fees and quarterly dues, which go to the expense account. Let us see how much has been collected under these two items. It costs members $5 admission fee, and $1 50 per quarter for dues. Consequently the five thousand two hundred and eighty members must have paid in $26,400 admission fees. As each one must pay the first quarterly dues in advance, one quarter's dues, or $7,920, must be added to the former amount, making a total of $34,320.

The league has been in existence one and one half years, or six quarters, and as one quarter has been reckoned, we must strike an average as to the amount paid in for the remaining five. Take half the present membership, or two thousand six hundred and forty, paying five quarters, at $1 50, and we get $19,800. Adding this to the former figures, we get a grand approximate total paid into the expense fund of the league of $54,120. Where is the published statement, which should be in the hands of every member of the league, showing what has been done with every dollar of this amount?

All the genuine, well-conducted fraternal insurance associations publish periodical statements, setting forth the receipts and disbursements in every fund down to the last cent. All moneys are paid out by a warrant on the Treasurer, and the date, number, amount, and purpose of each warrant is clearly set forth.

From what has come to my knowledge, I find that most of the proprietary endowment institutions keep their expense account under lock and key. In the annual report of the Secretary of the Pacific League is the following:

We, the undersigned Finance Committee, have made a careful examination of the books of the Secretary and Treasurer for the fiscal year 1888–89, and have found them correct in every particular.

J. MARTINS, Chairman.
J. H. STRUCKMEYER.
JAMES McALLISTER.

Following this is the sworn testimony as to the correctness of the accounts by an expert accountant. This is all, no doubt, very satisfactory to the perpetual nine Directors, but not to the remaining members of the " Pacific," who know as much about what has been done with their money as they do about the internal affairs of Timbuctoo. Where are the accounts which this finance committee certify to as correct? In all business undertakings, coöperative or otherwise, the financial statement is first submitted and the certificate as to its correctness follows. This is the cart without the horse.

FEASIBILITY OF ENDOWMENT PLANS.

The Secretary of the Pacific Endowment, in his report, instead of giving a statement of receipts and disbursements, sets forth an array of figures to prove the feasibility of the plan of the Pacific Endowment League. He puts the average rate of assessments at $2 25 a month, and the average coupon maturity at four years and one month. Each coupon amounts to $500.

The assessments, at $2 25 per month, amount to $27 per year, and in four years and one month will amount to $110 25. Consequently the Secretary, in his report, tries to prove how it is feasible to disburse $500 out of $110 25 receipts, or in other words, how he can pay out $4 50 for every dollar he takes in.

This is equivalent to a promise to pay about 300 per cent per annum upon the investment. What a run there would be on the savings banks of the State, with their insignificant 4 to 4½ per cent per annum, if the people placed any confidence in the glittering inducements held out by these bubble schemes. Unfortunately thousands of persons, chiefly women, are drawn into them. The butcher, baker, and grocer have often to suffer that these women may be able to pay their assessments. The Secretary of the Pacific Endowment League gives the receipts and obligations, by way of illustration, for two years 1890 and 1891, and then stops. Amazing results:

Receipts for the first eight months of 1890	$120,970 00
Excess of receipts during last four months of 1890	6,585 00
Excess of receipts during 1891	26,655 00
Total	$154,210 00

Why does he come to such a sudden halt? I will try to explain why he does so, by taking the Secretary precisely at his own averages of assessments and coupon maturity, and continue his calculation, precisely on the same lines, for two years and three months further. Let us see if the results will be as marvelous in producing hundreds of thousands of dollars surplus of receipts over disbursements as before.

Like the Secretary I will start out with six thousand members on the first day of January, 1890, and add to that number, the same as he does, one hundred and fifty new members each month. The problem then is simply this:

Six thousand members, January 1, 1890, at $2 25	$13,500 00
Six thousand one hundred and fifty members, February 1, 1890, at $2 25	13,837 50

And so on for four years and three months. Adding all together, we will get as follows:

First year	$184,275 00
Second year	232,875 00
Third year	281,475 00
Fourth year	330,075 00
First quarter of fifth year	90,112 50
Total	$1,118,812 50

This is the amount of receipts for assessments up to April 1, 1894. The organization would then have passed the sixth year of its existence, and the number of members on the roll, at the rate of increase figured upon, would have reached thirteen thousand five hundred. The Secretary states that four years and one month is the average, and six years the longest time it takes to mature a coupon. Consequently, at the lowest possible estimate, at least six thousand out of the thirteen thousand five hundred members on the roll must have had their coupons mature during these six years from the date of organization. From the start, and during all that period, the Pacific has been issuing certificates with coupons attached.

The coupons of six thousand members, at $500 each, would amount to $3,000,000, and the account would therefore stand:

Liabilities _____$3,000,000 00
Cash on hand _____ 1,118,812 50

Deficit_____$1,881,187 50

Instead of being able to pay to the members $4 50 for every dollar that they had paid in, the Pacific will not therefore be able to pay 40 cents on the dollar in 1894. The further along our calculations extend upon the same line the deeper will the Pacific sink in the mire of insolvency.

The history of all the defunct endowment associations shows that they usually give up the ghost a short time after the period when the average maturity of their coupons arrives.

Thousands of victims, then, are made to realize the truth of the universal law of political economy and finance, that enormous profits and small risks are conditions incompatible, and consequently non-existent.

FINANCIAL PROGRAMME OR PROMISES TO PAY.

The following table gives an interesting exhibit of the wonderful financial programme thrown out to catch the speculative eye of the man or woman who wants to make four or five dollars out of one. The assessment and maturity tables of a large number of these endowment associations, whether conducted on the fraternal or proprietary system, are so arranged that we can make comparisons on a unit of value, as in the following table. The average age of a member is taken at from thirty-four to thirty-five years, and the value of the coupon, $500. Where coupons are issued for a different sum, a calculation is made so as to bring the amount of assessment to cover $500. For example, where the coupon was for $200, two and a half times the assessments was figured on, and so on. Here are classed together the fraternal or coöperative and the proprietary; but, as I before pointed out, there is a wide line of demarkation between the two systems:

TABLE A.

Name of Organization.	Management.	Age of Members.	Amount of Coupon.	Period of Maturity.
1. Home Mutual Endowment Association	Proprietary	34 years 6 months	$500 00	2 years 9 months.
2. Golden Gate Endowment Association	Proprietary	Any age	500 00	3 years.
3. Mutual of Oakland Endowment Association	Proprietary	35 years	500 00	8 years.
4. Safety Endowment Association	Proprietary	35 years	500 00	2 years.
5. Fraternal Guild Endowment Association	Fraternal	Any age	500 00	3 years.
6. Self-Endowment Association	Proprietary	34 years 6 months	500 00	8 years.
7. Golden Shore Endowment Association	Fraternal	35 years	500 00	4 years.
8. National Endowment Association	Proprietary	Any age	500 00	1 year.
9. Royal Argosy Endowment Association	Fraternal	34 years 6 months	500 00	4 years.
10. Legon of the West Endowment Association	Fraternal	35 years	500 00	4 years.
11. Star of the West Endowment Association	Fraternal	35 years	500 00	4 years.
12. Guaranty Endowment Association	Proprietary	Any age	500 00	4 years.
13. Beacon Light Endowment Association	Fraternal	Any age	500 00	3 years.
14. Eureka Endowment Association	Proprietary	34 years 6 months	500 00	4 years.
15. United Endowment Associates	Fraternal	34 years 6 months	500 00	5 years 1½ months.
16. Pacific Endowment Association	Proprietary	34 years 6 months	500 00	4 years 1 month.
17. Bankers' Endowment Association	Proprietary	Any age	500 00	3 years.

TABLE A—Continued.

Name of Organization.	Monthly Assessments.	Total Amount Paid.	Per Cent of Profit.	Total Profit on the Dollar.	Total Profit on the Dollar Reduced to One Year.
1. Home Mutual Endowment Association	$9 40	$310 20	61	$1 61 for one dollar	$0 58
2. Golden Gate Endowment Association	6 00	237 60	110	2 10 for one dollar	70
3. Mutual of Oakland Endowment Association	2 32½	223 20	124	2 25 for one dollar, approximate	28
4. Safety Endowment Association	9 00	210 00	131	2 33⅓ for one dollar, approximate	1 15
5. Fraternal Guild Endowment Association	5 00	180 00	177	2 75 for one dollar, approximate	92
6. Self-Endowment Association	1 80	172 80	189	2 90 for one dollar	36
7. Golden Shore Endowment Association	3 00	168 00	197	3 00 for one dollar, approximate	74
8. National Endowment Association	12 50	150 00	233	3 33⅓ for one dollar, approximate	3 33
9. Royal Argosy Endowment Association	3 00	144 00	247	3 50 for one dollar, approximate	86
10. Legion of the West Endowment Association	3 00	144 00	247	3 50 for one dollar, approximate	86
11. Star of the West Endowment Association	2 00	144 00	247	3 50 for one dollar, approximate	86
12. Guaranty Endowment Association	2 75	132 00	278	3 75 for one dollar, approximate	94
13. Beacon Light Endowment Association	3 50	126 00	296	4 00 for one dollar, approximate	1 32
14. Eureka Endowment Association	2 58	123 84	303	4 00 for one dollar, approximate	1 00
15. United Endowment Associates	1 80	110 70	351	4 50 for one dollar, approximate	88
16. Pacific Endowment Association	2 25	110 25	353	4 50 for one dollar, approximate	1 11
17. Bankers' Endowment Association	2 50	90 00	455	5 50 for one dollar, approximate	1 85

HOW MUCH ON THE DOLLAR?

In the following Table (B) the total profit on the dollar contained in Table (A) is divided by the period of maturity and reduced to the total profit on the dollar in one year. This will give us a unit of value which will clearly set forth the relative gains promised by the different associations enumerated. The progressive arrangement would then be as follows:

TABLE B.

NAME OF ORGANIZATION.	Profit on One Dollar Reduced to One Year.
Mutual Endowment, Oakland	$0 28
Self-Endowment, San Francisco	36
Home Mutual Endowment, San Francisco	58
Golden Gate Endowment, San Francisco	71
Golden Shore Endowment, San Francisco	74
Royal Argosy Endowment, San Francisco	86
Legion of the West Endowment, San Francisco	86
Star of the West Endowment, San Francisco	86
United Endowment Associates, San Francisco	88
Fraternal Guild Endowment, San Francisco	92
Guaranty Endowment, San Francisco	94
Eureka Endowment, San Francisco	1 00
Pacific Endowment, San Francisco	1 11
Safety Endowment, San Francisco	1 15
Beacon Light Endowment, San Francisco	1 32
Bankers' Endowment, San Francisco	1 85
National Endowment, San Francisco	3 33

DISPARITY IN CONTRACTS.

If we had no other criterion to go by, the remarkable disparity in the financial programmes of these endowment concerns should be in itself sufficient to create distrust. Take any line of business—commercial, financial, old line insurance, etc.—and inquire if such differences exist in the quotations of rival firms or corporations? A few cents or a small fraction of a dollar is generally the rule. Among the endowments, one man joins the Mutual of Oakland, and pays in assessments for eight years at $2 32½ per month, or $223 20, and receives $500 for his first coupon. If he had joined the National, and paid in $2 50 per month for the same time, or $240, he would be entitled to receive $800. A difference in assessments of only $16 80, but a difference in amount of coupons cashed of $300.

The Mutual Endowment of Oakland, according to the foregoing table, holds out the lowest inducements of profit among the endowment schemes. Only 124 per cent, after the lapse of eight years, on the total amount paid in for assessments—$2 24 for every dollar paid in, or 28 cents per annum. The Pacific promises to give twice as much as the Mutual in about half the time, which is equivalent to giving four times the value for money paid into its treasury. It will give $1 11 for every 28 cents given by the Mutual. If any dependence were to be placed in the promises of these endowment concerns, it is plain that an investor would select the one which promises the most. Who would go to Oakland to invest his money when he could do four times as well in San Francisco? Who would wait eight years to realize 110 per cent upon an investment in the Mutual, when he could get 233 per cent in one year in the National?

33

COMPARISONS BETWEEN ENDOWMENTS AND SAVINGS BANKS.

When a person reads of profits running from 61 to 455 per cent, how insignificant must appear the 4¼ or 4½ per cent per annum allowed by the savings banks.

Take for example the Pacific Endowment, whose average maturity of coupon is four years and one month and the average assessment $2 25. For the payment of $110 25 a member receives $500. How much would he get instead if he had deposited the same amount monthly in a savings bank in San Francisco?

Suppose he would receive 5 per cent per annum, which is higher than current rates. For the first six months he would deposit $13 50 and receive no interest. At the end of the year he would have $27, and interest for six months on $13 50, or 33 cents, making a total of $27 33. Second year he would get interest at the end of six months amounting to 68 cents; total principal and interest, $40 83. Continuing the calculation, at the end of the four years and one month the depositor would be entitled to draw from the savings banks $119 40. A comparison between the Pacific Endowment Association and a savings bank, both of San Francisco, would be as follows:

	Pacific Endowment.	Savings Bank.
Deposit	$110 25	$110 25
Profit	389 75	9 15
Total	$500 00	$119 40

An investor, therefore, who could only gain $9 15 in a savings bank, would, by investing his money in the Pacific Endowment, gain $389 75, or more than forty times as much.

Is it not remarkable that with such stupendous inducements our savings banks are not depleted of their millions by breathless depositors? Sensible people pause and ask the questions: How can an endowment association give four or five dollars for one, while a savings bank can add only four or five cents to the same. Where is the money to come from? Is it not the fact that these very endowments actually deposit their surplus money and reserve funds in the savings banks? Their legitimate profit or gain consequently comes from the small rate of interest allowed by the savings banks, and yet they promise their membership forty or fifty times this amount.

AVERAGE PROFITS IN ENDOWMENTS.

The endowments in San Francisco having the largest membership are the United Endowment Associates, Legion of the West, Royal Argosy, Golden Shore, and Fraternal Guild, conducted on the fraternal or lodge plan, and the Pacific, Eureka, Guaranty, and Safety on the proprietary or self-constituted, self-perpetuating-in-office system.

The average total gain per annum on the dollar in the fraternal organizations is 85 cents, and in the proprietary $1 25.

The average period, in round numbers, in which coupons will mature in the former is four years, and in the latter three years and six months.

The length of time which it takes for a coupon to mature is of vast importance to these associations. The shorter the time the fewer the lapses,

3-L

and, consequently, the larger the number who will demand payment of their coupons.

The success of endowment associations depends upon two contingencies:
1. The number of members who lapse in their payments and lose all they had paid in.
2. The number of new members added from day to day.

In the event of one or both of these failing the organization collapses. As I remarked in my report on the so called national building and loan associations, the division òf profits derived from the lapses of members is somewhat analogous to the division of loot by bushwhackers after a raid. The healthy growth of the endowments depends, therefore, upon the amount of loot or booty left behind by the unfortunates who have lapsed on the one hand and the amount of coin in the pockets of those coming in on the other.

The organization scrapes into its treasure box what is left by the fellow who has gone out the back door with pockets empty, and joyfully welcomes the dollars of the one coming in the front door with pockets full.

LAPSES OR FORFEITURES.

Loot or lapsed money is required to pay off the coupons past due, and the fresh supply is necessary to keep the ball rolling. Where the period of maturity is long the lapses are large.

Here is the great difference between the reckoning of lapses as applied to insurance and endowment institutions. In a life insurance company the period is *indefinite*, in the endowment it is *definite*. A person in the former very often, after paying his premium for years, gets tired of doing so and drops off, or else, from some cause, he is unable to pay. As a result the entire membership of an insurance company changes every eight or nine years.

In an endowment, on the contrary, a member having to pay his assessments for a definite and, generally, short period, will make desperate efforts to keep up his payments until the maturity of the first coupon. After that he generally drops out and thinks himself " mighty lucky."

In the Safety Endowment of San Francisco, for instance, a man becoming a member at thirty-five years of age has to pay assessments for two years only, when his coupon matures. It is easy to see two years ahead, and no sensible man will join the Safety unless he feels safe about his payments for these two short years. Lapses, therefore, will be exceedingly rare.

On the other hand, take the Mutual of Oakland, in which a man of the same age will have to continue his payment of assessments, month after month, for eight years before he can get his coupon cashed, and the lapses will be remarkably large.

The Secretary of the Mutual informs me that, out of a total on the roll of membership of less than two thousand three hundred, more than a thousand, or nearly 50 per cent, have lapsed. As the organization has been in existence only five years it is likely that 75 per cent of the membership will lapse by the end of the eight years.

The probabilities of an organization like the Mutual of Oakland fulfilling its obligations are proportionately greater therefore than those having a shorter time in which their coupons mature. This is made clear by the fact that it has been enabled to lay by a large reserve fund.

It was given in evidence before me that one of the reasons why the

Occidental Endowment had collapsed was because those who had received cash for their coupons did not continue their membership. They but follow the dictates of human nature. Most of those who become members of endowment associations like the Occidental, do so as a matter of pure speculation, and if they are so fortunate as to draw a prize, put it in their pocket and walk off. Having got four or five times the value of their money, they are not so foolish as to contribute to the same results for others who follow. It is simply a game of grab. Take the plan of the Pacific Endowment, as shown before, for an illustration. At the end of the first six years of its existence, it would find itself bankrupt, unless it had either trebled the monthly assessments, or two thirds of the six thousand members, whose coupons would fall due, had lapsed or forfeited their claims. If a business house having a large number of customers could not keep itself on a paying basis without a continuous addition to the number, what would be said of it? The entire system rests on an unsound basis, for it is simply "robbing Peter to pay Paul."

THE SAFETY.

From a circular issued by the Safety Endowment Union, the following list.is taken, showing the amount received and disbursed to the members therein named:

Claim No.	Coupon No.	NAMES OF MEMBERS MATURING COUPONS.	Residence.	Date of Maturing.	Amount of Assessment Paid.	No. of Endowment Certificate	Amount Coupon Payable.
1	1	Holmes, M. P.	San Francisco.	July 16, 1889	$60 00	19	$250
2	1	Holmes, Mrs. A. W.	San Francisco.	Aug. 7, 1889	61 60	6	250
3	1	Skillicorn, John	San Francisco.	Aug. 13, 1889	66 50	48	250
4	1	Graham, Mrs. M. A.	San Francisco.	Aug. 25, 1889	70 00	72	250
5	1	Williamson, Mrs. C. A.	San Francisco.	Aug. 27, 1889	66 50	70	250
6	1	Putnam, Mrs. Martha.	San Francisco.	Sept. 10, 1889	76 00	92	250
7	1	Shaughnessy, Martin.	San Francisco.	Sept. 12, 1889	60 90	42	250
8	1	Rebut, Armand	San Francisco.	Sept. 12, 1889	76 00	63	250
9	1	McDonnell, Patrick	Vallejo	Sept. 14, 1889	76 00	79	250
10	1	Bischoff, Henry	San Francisco.	Sept. 14, 1889	76 00	112	250
11	1	Angus, D. M.	Vallejo	Sept. 16, 1889	76 00	123	250
12	1	Dawson, John	Vallejo	Sept. 21, 1889	66 50	99	250
13	1	Dawson, Mrs. Rose	Vallejo	Sept. 23, 1889	66 50	105	250
14	1	Houseman,Mrs.Louisa.	Vallejo	Sept. 23, 1889	76 00	130	250
15	1	Wickham, Mrs. Mary	Napa	Sept. 25, 1889	80 00	158	250
16	1	Gordon, Mrs. Mary	San Francisco.	Sept. 26, 1889	70 40	64	250
17	1	Trull, F. W.	Vallejo	Sept. 28, 1889	76 00	129	250
18	1	Byars, E. G.	Napa	Sept. 29, 1889	80 00	180	250
19	1	Bogle, Mrs. E. A.	San Francisco.	Sept. 30, 1889	70 40	71	250
20	1	Meissner, Carl	San Francisco.	Oct. 5, 1889	56 00	8	250
21	1	Smith, Peter A.	San Francisco.	Oct. 5, 1889	85 50	189	250
22	1	Morrow, John C.	San Francisco.	Oct. 6, 1889	90 00	191	250
23	1	Hunt, H. B.	San Francisco.	Oct. 9, 1889	67 50	30	250
24	1	McKee, J. L.	San Francisco.	Oct. 12, 1889	63 00	1	250
25	1	McLaughlin,Mrs.M.A.	San Francisco.	Oct. 12, 1889	90 00	215	250
26	1	Donovan, Patrick	Vallejo	Oct. 12, 1889	67 50	28	250
27	1	MacKeever, Mrs. L. B.	San Francisco.	Oct. 14, 1889	79 20	134	250
28	1	Cassidy, Wm.	San Francisco.	Oct. 14, 1889	85 50	172	250
29	1	Wiese, K. R.	San Francisco.	Oct. 14, 1889	85 50	225	250
30	1	Cass, Mrs. Mary E.	Vallejo	Oct. 15, 1889	72 00	46	250
31	1	Fairweather, A. J.	San Francisco.	Oct. 16, 1889	90 00	234	250
32	1	Ackerman, Mrs. J. C.	San Francisco.	Oct. 16, 1889	85 50	229	250
33	1	Stone, Mrs. Jane	San Lorenzo	Oct. 19, 1889	85 50	209	250
34	1	Doran, Richard	San Francisco.	Oct. 19, 1889	90 00	245	250
35	1	Dannenfelzer, Mrs. A.	San Francisco	Oct. 20, 1889	67 50	41	250
36	1	Seeley, C. B.	Napa	Oct. 21, 1889	79 20	208	250
37	1	Hall, Mrs. E. L.	San Francisco.	Oct. 22, 1889	85 50	224	250

Claim No.	Coupon No.	Names of Members Maturing Coupons.	Residence.	Date of Maturing.	Amount of Assessment Paid.	No. of Endowment Certificate	Amount Coupon Payable.
38	1	Tobey, N. G.	San Francisco.	Oct. 23, 1889 ..	$85 50	257	$250
39	1	Conklin, Mrs. Jane	San Francisco.	Oct. 24, 1889 ..	79 20	119	250
40	1	Philips, T. K.	San Francisco.	Oct. 26, 1889 ..	63 00	14	250
41	1	McClure, Wm.	San Francisco.	Oct. 27, 1889 ..	90 00	259	250
42	1	Graves, W. H. H.	Oakland	Oct. 28, 1889 ..	62 10	4	250
43	1	Earl, Mrs. F. N.	Napa	Oct. 28, 1889 ..	79 20	183	250
44	1	Wiese, G. H.	San Francisco.	Oct. 29, 1889 ..	85 50	242	250
45	1	Gerbes, Mrs. R.	San Francisco.	Oct. 30, 1889 ..	85 50	243	250
46	1	Wescott, Mrs. E. S.	Rocklin	Oct. 31, 1889 ..	90 00	274	250
		Totals			$3,496 20		$11,500

From the foregoing list, it can be seen that $11,500 was disbursed to members from whom only $3,496 20 was received, or nearly $3 33⅓ was paid for $1 received. The Safety was organized June 28, 1888, and was therefore nearly one year and four months in existence on the last listed date. Two hundred per cent per annum on an investment is not bad, at a time when capital is ready to grasp at anything that will return from five to ten.

HOW CAN THE SCHEME BE WORKED?

But here the query comes in, how can this be done, and *how can it continue to be done?* A person can easily understand how, as long as cash comes pouring in for new certificates of membership, the problem can be worked satisfactorily for the managers, but like the Occidental and the numerous other defunct endowments in the long mortuary list already given, the inevitable collapse is sure to come, leaving countless mourners behind.

The stereotyped reply given to all this is that people go into these schemes with their eyes open, and if they suffer they must stand the consequences. The speculator knows, it is said, what risks he takes, and cannot " squeal " if he should be pinched. All of this will equally apply to the people who invest in lottery tickets, and yet the law steps in and says that these tickets shall not be peddled or sold in California. Any one caught violating the law is punished. If it is right to protect the public from loss by speculation in the one case, why not in the other? The dealers in Louisiana lottery tickets must pursue their illegal calling in hidden paths, but the theorists, in endowment schemes which promise three or four dollars for one, defend the feasibility of such schemes in the public press, and hold up their heads on a level with the legitimate business men of the community.

THE PROPRIETARY AND FRATERNAL COMPARED.

Here lies the remarkable point of difference between the proprietary and fraternal methods of endowment associations. The United Endowment Associates, the Royal Argosy, and the Legion of the West promptly filled out the blank forms sent from this office. Free access to their books and papers was cheerfully granted. Scrutiny of their affairs was not needed, as they publish, in full detail, at least annually, the receipts and disbursements of all moneys, no matter what the fund to which they belong.

The intimate knowledge of the financial condition and operations of the organization begets confidence on the part of the membership and gives it strength to surmount difficulties.

THE UNITED ENDOWMENT ASSOCIATES.

The United Endowment Associates was organized at Napa City, California, August 23, 1884. It has over sixty lodges, a few of which are outside the State, embracing a membership of more than five thousand. Up to the last day of August, 1889, it had paid out on matured coupons $152,875, out of a total of disbursements amounting to $165,500. It admits to membership white persons of both sexes between the ages of eighteen and fifty. It pays endowments during life of members of one eighth of one of five classes of certificates, from $1,000 to $5,000 inclusive, in one eighth of life expectancy (from age at time of joining to seventy-five years old), and in case of death *only* the next coupon due thereafter immediately, collected by assessment of graded rates according to the age at the time of joining on the membership of the entire Order. The endowment fund is controlled by the Grand Lodge.

Up to and including October 1, 1889, thirty-one assessments, averaging $2 40, were levied, which is an average of six assessments a year for the five years and one month it has been in existence. There were levied one assessment in 1885, four in 1886, eight in 1887, nine in 1888, and nine up to October in 1889.

The following table shows the membership, etc., from the date of organization:

YEAR.	No. of Members.	No. of Assessments.	No. of Deaths.	Amount Paid on Deaths In Full.	No. of Coupons Matured and Paid.	Amount Paid on Coupons Matured in Full.	Total Disbursements.
Aug. 23 to—							
Dec. 31, 1884..	200	1					
Dec. 31, 1885..	456	1	2	$1,000 00			$1,000 00
Dec. 31, 1886..	842	4	6	3,125 00			3,125 00
Dec. 31, 1887..	2,269	8	5	3,000 00	44	$24,875 00	27,875 00
Dec. 31, 1888..	4,360	9	23	13,625 00	83	48,875 00	62,500 00
Aug. 31, 1889..	5,030	7	21	11,875 00	103	59,125 00	71,000 00
Totals......	5,030	30	57	$32,625 00	230	$132,875 00	$165,500 00

From the report of the Secretary it appears that one hundred and seventy coupons, amounting to $104,125, will have matured during the year 1889. For the year following (1890), the coupons maturing will amount to $228,500. Unless, therefore, the membership should largely increase, the number of assessments to be levied will be about double in 1890 what they were in 1889. There is no reserve fund to draw upon, unless the sum received from one assessment can be so considered. The success of an organization of this character depends upon a continued increase in the membership. New blood is absolutely required to stand the strain of increasing assessments. The increase for the first few years of the United Associates was remarkably good. For the year 1889, while not up to the mark of former years, it was still large. The number, however, must not lag, but keep on increasing, or assessments must be increased.

In order to pay $228,500 for maturing coupons in 1891, there will be required ninety-five thousand two hundred and eight individual assessments, at the average of $2 40 each.

If the membership increased so as to average six thousand in 1891, it will require about sixteen assessments to meet the liabilities on account of coupons maturing.

THE LEGION OF THE WEST.

Next to the United Endowment Associates comes the Legion of the West, which was incorporated September 8, 1885. According to the report of the Secretary for 1889 it had twenty-nine lodges, and a membership of two thousand four hundred and twenty-seven, on July 1, 1889. The plan of this organization is outlined in its prospectus as follows:

The Grand Lodge is composed of its officers, duly elected, standing committees, and representatives from subordinate lodges, and holds annual sessions. From this body emanate all laws for the government of the Order, and subject to the laws, it controls the funds.

Subordinate lodges act as custodians of the special benefit and beneficiary moneys until called by the officers of the Grand Lodge; they have charge of the administration of their local affairs, with power to accept or reject those who may apply for membership.

TWO DISTINCT CLASSES OF MEMBERS.

First—A. Special benefit members of first series, contributing to the special benefit fund and holding certificates, with coupons attached, payable to the member at stated periods during life, and in case of death, one coupon being payable to the member's nominee.

B. Special benefit members of second series, contributing to the special benefit fund, and holding certificates with ten coupons attached, payable as they mature, to the member if living, or if dead, to his nominee.

(Several special benefit certificates will be issued to a member, as hereinafter stated.)

Second—Beneficiary members, contributing to the beneficiary fund, and holding beneficiary certificates, payable only at death to nominees to be named.

Membership in the special benefit class does not affect membership in the beneficiary class, nor can the funds of either of said two classes be used for the payment of claims against the other.

Special benefit certificates of the first series are divided into six classes, viz.: Class 1, $1,000; Class 2, $2,000; Class 3, $3,000; Class 4, $4,000; Class 5, $5,000; Class 6, $6,000. Ten coupons being attached to each certificate, except to persons over fifty years of age, when coupons will be attached as follows:

```
Age 51-------------------------------------------------8 coupons.
Age 52-------------------------------------------------8 coupons.
Age 53-------------------------------------------------7 coupons.
Age 54-------------------------------------------------6 coupons.
```

Certificates of this series will be issued to members of sound bodily health, between the ages of fifteen and fifty-five years.

For the fiscal year ending July 31, 1889, there were $52,126 30 collected in assessments, $47,608 12 of which was apportioned to pay maturing endowment coupons, and $1,911 84 for death claims. The remainder, $2,606 28, went to the general or expense account.

There were six endowment assessments levied during the year, averaging $3 92 each, or $23 52 for the year. There were balances on hand in the three funds of the Legion as follows:

```
Beneficiary fund ------------------------------------------------ $180 22
Endowment fund ------------------------------------------------ 49,655 46
Expense fund -------------------------------------------------- 2,086 14

Total -------------------------------------------------------- $51,921 82
```

For the year ending July 31, 1889, there was paid a total for death benefits of $12,221 13 out of the two funds called beneficiary and special benefit.

No coupons had matured during the said fiscal year. The Secretary, in his report, shows that by the end of next year—1890—coupons will have matured amounting to $193,483 33.

The number of assessments to be levied has been increased from six during the past fiscal year to ten for the present. Next year the number will be still further increased, and they will have to keep on increasing year after year under its present system.

THE ROYAL ARGOSY.

The Royal Argosy was organized in San Francisco, May 23, 1888, and on October 1, 1889, had thirty-five lodges, with a membership of two thousand one hundred. It is not incorporated.

The plans and purposes of the Royal Argosy are as follows:

1. To unite fraternally all white persons of good moral character, who are socially acceptable, and, if for beneficial membership, of sound bodily health, between the ages of fifteen and sixty-five years.
2. To establish a Protection Degree (Class A) Fund, from which, on the satisfactory evidence of the death of a beneficial member of the Order of the Protection Degree, who has complied with all its lawful requirements, a sum not exceeding $5,000 shall be paid to the family, orphans, dependents, or other beneficiaries, as the member may direct; and the further sum of an amount not exceeding $250 (on account of the certificate held by the member) to each of the two members holding valid certificates numbered anterior and subsequent to the certificate of the member deceased.
3. To establish an Aid Degree (Class B) Fund for the payment of an aid certificate, with ten coupons attached, and no coupon to exceed in amount the sum of $700 (said coupons being payable at stated periods, the amount of the next maturing coupon ONLY being payable in case of the death of the member) to the family, orphans, dependents, or other beneficiaries, as the members may direct.
4. To establish a Relief Degree (Class C) Fund, from which, on the satisfactory evidence of the sickness of a beneficial member of the Relief Degree, a sum not exceeding $20 per week shall be paid to such member for a period of twenty-six weeks.
5. To establish a Reserve Fund for the benefit of such members of the Order in good standing of the different degrees who have been contributing members thereof for not less than five years, thereby limiting the extent of their liabilities and the number of assessments to be paid per annum.
6. To educate its members socially, morally, and intellectually.
7. To extend all moral and material aid in its power to members and to those dependent on them.

FORMATION OF THE ORDER.

The Supreme Lodge is the supreme head of the Order, and is composed of its organizers and associates, officers, and representatives from Grand Lodges. Its regular meetings are held annually, and special sessions may be called by the Supreme President at the request of five or more members.

Grand Lodges are composed of representatives from each subordinate lodge in the State, and are governed by such officers and committees as they may annually elect. Subordinate lodges are placed within their control and supervision, subject to the laws of the Supreme Lodge.

Subordinate lodges are composed of Protection, Aid, and Relief Degree or beneficial, non-beneficial, and honorary members of good social and moral standing, who are admitted upon petition by ballot. All petitioners for beneficial membership must be of sound bodily health, and between the ages of fifteen and sixty-five years. Non-beneficial members are persons acceptable to every member of the lodge, but ineligible to beneficiary membership on account of age, unsound health, or other causes, or who may desire to enter the Order as such; they pay no assessments, and are not entitled to any moneyed benefits from the Order. Honorary members may be elected unanimously by one lodge from members of another lodge as a mark of esteem and respect for special services rendered to a lodge or to the Order at large.

DUES AND BENEFITS.

Each member pays as quarterly dues such an amount as may be agreed upon by the lodge, but cannot be less than 50 cents per quarter.

EXPENSES OF GOVERNMENT.

Each subordinate lodge pays a per capita tax of 10 cents per month per member (for the time they are members) to the Supreme Lodges; Grand Lodges receive 80 per cent of the per capita tax collected from lodges within their jurisdiction. From the amount received, the mileage of representatives, salaries, expenses of annual sessions, and incidentals are paid.

SALARIED OFFICERS.

Salaries are paid to those of the supreme officers who perform the work necessary for the Order, and the amount is determined by the Supreme Lodge in session.

FUNDS AND THEIR SECURITY.

All moneys are received by Supreme Accountant. All officers of the Order who have charge of any of its funds are required to give sufficient bonds for the faithful discharge of their duties. These bonds may be increased, from time to time, as the numerical strength of the Order increases.

The total income from assessments up to October 1, 1889, amounted to $22,653 24. There was paid for death claims, Class B, $3,500. The Royal Argosy has over $20,000 of a reserve fund.

ENDOWMENTS ON TRIAL.

It is the practice, whenever any attempt is made to prove the infeasibility of their plans, for the officers of endowment associations to point to the long continued success of the Ancient Order of United Workmen, Knights of Honor, Chosen Friends, and others.

There is a deep line of demarkation between the two classes. Both in one respect are alike—that is, in insuring their members and paying the policy on the assessment plan—but the endowments propose to pay it in installments to the living members, while the Workmen, Knights of Honor, etc., only do so to the legatee after death.

The supporters of the endowment mutual assessment system then, in order to inspire confidence, must be able to point to the examples of an association conducted upon their plan which has been attended with success for a period long enough to give fair assurance of stability. This they are as yet unable to do. The United Endowment Associates stands beyond question at the head of the mutual or assessment endowment associations in California. It has been in successful operation for more than five years. It has a large membership; has paid a large sum for coupons; has been economically managed, and has the advantage of having at its helm capable and energetic officers. The United Endowment has then all the elements of success, if success is possible.

The association is on its trial, for as none of the mutual endowments are six years old, it is but an experiment so far. It would indeed be astonishing if it could succeed in continuing to pay 88 cents on the dollar per year, whilst the Mutual Endowment of Oakland, conducted on the company plan, can afford to pay only 28 cents.

The endowment feature of insurance of itself is not new. It has been in operation for many years by old insurance companies, but as was demonstrated by Mr. Bacon in his testimony, there is a wide divergence between the old and the new methods.

THE OLD LINE SYSTEM OF ENDOWMENT.

In the old line insurance companies the endowment plan may be considered limited payment life policies, which provide for the payment of definite cash surrender values at the end of certain periods defined. The plan usually embraces the payment of the full amount of the face of the policy to the heirs or legatee of the insured in case of death, at any time, from the day the policy was issued. Take the rates of five of them, by way of example, for an endowment policy for $1,000, payable in ten years, or in the event of death, to an insurer thirty-five years of age:

Northwestern of Milwaukee ....$102 51 annual premium.
Manhattan of New York...$105 53 annual premium.
Washington of New York...$105 53 annual premium.
Pacific of California...$105 53 annual premium.
Equitable of New York . ...$105 53 annual premium.

In contrasting these rates with those charged by our " coöperative " local endowments, the first thing to strike the reader will be the remarkable uniformity in the amount of the annual payments charged by the regular or old line companies. In our San Francisco born endowment institutions, as described, the rates have been fixed and plans adopted in a helter-skelter, razzle-dazzle style.

The projectors would appear to have entered upon a "go-as-you-please" race for public patronage.

The next point of distinction between the old and the new is in the amount of money to be paid for the endowment. The assessments charged by our new style locals are a mere bagatelle compared to the old rates. Instead of a man getting four or five dollars for one at the end of three or four years, he actually has paid in more than he receives when his endowment matures in the old companies. For instance, in the case of four out of five of the examples before given, he will have paid in to the company $1,055 30 when the time arrives when he is to receive $1,000 in return. Of course it should be borne in mind that during all that period his life was insured for $1,000.

WHY SHOULD NOT THE NEW SYSTEM SUCCEED.

But apart from these discrepancies—glaring and significant as they are—there is nothing which can be successfully done under proprietary or company management, which should not be accomplished with at least as good results and at less expense by coöperators. This fact has been demonstrated by the wonderful success attending the experiment of insuring the lives of their members by fraternal societies or orders, whose membership now runs up to the hundreds of thousands. If successful in insurance on the entire *life*, why not in *stated periods or divisions* of life, is a question which may reasonably be asked.

If coöperators have not only held their ground but got the best of the old system in the one case, why not in the other? If, then, a genuine coöperative organization finds that its plans are not feasible, or that it promises more than it can fulfill, it rests with itself to alter said plans so as to bring them within the range of practicability.

In such an organization all members stand precisely upon the same level, with an equal voice and vote in its affairs.

There are no perpetual or life term officials. High salaries and other extravagances are not tolerated. Their annual meetings and election of officers are not shams. Whether they gain or lose, sink or swim, is their own affair. The great difficulty is to discriminate between the genuine and the counterfeit coöperative. Not every one that has supreme, grand, and subordinate lodges, with the usual staff of supreme and grand officers, is a genuine fraternal organization. "Not every one that says 'Lord! Lord?' shall enter into the Kingdom of Heaven." In some of the so called "orders" it will be found that the supreme lodge is in the hands of a self-constituted, self-perpetuating coterie, who were the prime movers in organizing the order and who manage its affairs to suit themselves. You will generally find in the constitution of the "order" some section or clause by means of which these people can hold on to power. They fill the offices and control the finances. Their coupons are among the first to mature, and their friends are the first to be taken care of. The true ring can be best ascertained by studying their laws, and from the proceedings at the annual meetings and the results shown in the reports of the various officers. The law of the State should define what constitutes a " coöperative fraternal or benevolent association," and put it in the power of the State Insurance Commissioner to suppress any not coming up to the standard.

In a genuine coöperative endowment, where the members frequently meet to discuss ways and means for the good of the Order, social attachments are formed which a member will desire to maintain regardless of pecuniary considerations. Hence it follows that members in them do not, to the same extent as in the proprietary organizations, drop off after receiving cash for the first coupon. They take a personal interest in the success of the league, and contribute, at least for a time, their share that the men and women of their lodge whom they meet night after night may be as successful as themselves.

A simple arithmetical demonstration of the non-feasibility of their plans is of itself not conclusive evidence that an endowment coöperative association will collapse when it has within itself such elements of recuperation. While all fair minded citizens must condemn the false pretensions and dubious methods of the proprietary endowment companies organized for the special benefit of a few individuals, it is but right and proper to give the genuine coöperative endowment associations a fair trial before pronouncing condemnation. At the same time, sham fraternals should be mercilessly stamped out of existence. They are a reproach and a menace to the genuine organizations.

CONCLUSION.

In conclusion I desire to express my sincere conviction, based upon the developments of this investigation, that the coöperative feature of endowment insurance is antagonistic to the true idea of what coöperation means to accomplish.

Sterling coöperation is an incentive to thrift, teaching that the bettering of one's condition must be brought about by economy, and that what tends to saving is a recognized blessing. The endowment schemes, on the contrary, as here conducted, hold out the idea that the prizes, in the lottery of life, are more inviting than the few cents on the dollar of coöperative saving.

Thrift is subordinated to luck, and the wage earner is invited to throw his hard earned dollars into the endowment wheel of fortune, upon the chance of drawing a prize. Their motto is to *make* and not to *save* money— to reach fortune by a "Royal" road, instead of by the old "Industry and Thrift" highway.

In another way endowment insurance is repulsive to the proper conception of coöperation. Coöperation means mutuality—common support, working together for the common good. It teaches that what is good for the individual is for the good of all, and what works to the injury of the one is an injury to the whole body.

Success in the endowment insurance depends to a great extent upon the lapsed or forfeited payments of members. The gain to some is therefore taken from the pockets of others, and it is the experience in such schemes that the small few are the gainers, while the great many are the losers. The man who falls by the wayside in the endowment associations, instead of being helped to his feet by his brother coöperators, has his pockets rifled of what little he had paid into the common fund. A member can realize profits only at the expense of his friends and neighbors in the same association.

⸺ Endowment associations, therefore, in every form—proprietary, fraternal, guild, or lodge—are based upon principles inimical to the teachings of true coöperation, and in their practices and results are likely to work injury to the cause.

JOHN J. TOBIN,
Commissioner.

INQUIRY INTO THE PRACTICES AND PURPOSES OF ENDOWMENT ASSOCIATIONS.

JOHN J. TOBIN, Commissioner.

BUREAU OF LABOR STATISTICS, September 23, 1889.

Mr. Carl Spelling appeared for the State Labor Bureau.

R. E. COLLINS,

Of San José, a Director of the Western Mutual Benefit Association, called as a witness and sworn.

MR. SPELLING: Were you one of the organizers of the Western Mutual Benefit Association? Answer—Yes.

Q. Tell who organized it, and about what time? A. I think that we got ready for business—I could not name the date exactly—but I think it was about the first of May when we sent out the circulars.

COLONEL TOBIN: The first of May of this year? A. Yes.

MR. SPELLING: Did you incorporate; that is, did the Western Mutual incorporate? A. We did.

Q. Did you incorporate previously to the time of sending out the circulars? A. Yes.

Q. How long previous had you incorporated? A. I could not tell—two or three days or a week. It might have been two weeks. We were incorporated before we attempted to do any business. That was our position.

Q. Did Mr. Riddle or Mr. Brookes confer with you in regard to the organization of the Western Mutual? A. Mr. Riddle did.

Q. Did you not talk about it to Mr. Brookes, the President of the Occidental? A. No, sir.

COLONEL TOBIN: Who were Riddle and Brookes? A. They were President and Vice-President of the Occidental.

Q. Did they first meet and associate in the organization of the Western Mutual? A. I do not know that that is the fact.

Q. Was not the object of that organization to continue and carry out the objects of that association—the Occidental—in part? A. No, sir; it was not. That was in the matter nothing at all.

Q. To what class of persons did you send the first batch of circulars sent out? A. Chiefly sent to Occidental members to give them the chance to insure in the new organization, or reinsure themselves, if they so desired.

Q. Did you send circulars to all the members of the Occidental, or to only a part? A. All. They were sent to all as far as I know. That was my intention.

Q. How do you know that they were sent to all the members or any members of the association? A. Simply, that was the instruction given, to have the circular sent to each one of the Occidental.

Q. How did you determine who were members of the Occidental? A. That I cannot tell; we had no way of knowing.

Q. You say the Directors of the Western Mutual were yourself, A. M. Pollock, Dr. M. S. Logan, C. Leshir, and F. F. Morelli? A. Yes.

Q. They were the Directors and also the incorporators? A. Yes.

Q. Were not all those incorporators—members—certificate holders in the Occidental? A. I do not know.

Q. You were? A. I was.

Q. Was not Mr. Pollock? A. I never asked him.

Q. Do you know where he is? A. I do not know.

Q. Did you not belong in this? A. I did, but I do not.

Q. Was not Mr. Leshir a member of the Occidental? A. I could not tell.

Q. Mr. Morelli? A. Mr. Morelli was a member.

Q. He is not President? A. Secretary.

Q. Are you President? A. I am.

Q. Mr. Pollock was first President? A. Yes.

Q. In the first circular that you sent out did you not refer expressly to the Occidental and its collapse as the reason for the organization of the Western Mutual? A. I think it was the object.

Q. Then the object of incorporating the Western Mutual was to succeed the Occidental? A. Not to succeed at all. It was to organize a new organization on a different plan.

Q. It was to be organized with the members of the Occidental as a basis? A. Our idea was to get material wherever we could; and naturally knowing that there was a quantity of members out of insurance, we supposed, of course, we could get material there.

Q. Did you organize it before the collapse of the Occidental, and send out your circulars? A. Not before; after the collapse.

Q. Where did you get the list of the members? A. That I do not know. I was not President.

Q. Did you not see the first list? A. I never saw the list from that day to this.

Q. Is that one of the circulars you sent out? A. That is one of the circulars, April fifteenth. We don't deny it.

Colonel Tobin: Was your plan somewhat similar to the plan of the Occidental? A. No, sir; it was on the assessment plan; no comparison with the Occidental plan.

Q. Did it not embrace somewhat the same plan as the Occidental? A. No, sir; no comparison.

Q. Did your plan not divide into four different assessments? A. No, sir. This plan is not.

Mr. Spelling. Mr. Commissioner, I want to examine that circular (April fifteenth). It is offered in evidence.

Mr. Spelling: What is the membership? A. I do not know that.

Q. Do you know when that proposition you made to members of the Occidental was first published, that you sent out? A. I think it is embraced there. That is all I know. There were several circulars sent; of course, I cannot tell the purport of them; they speak for themselves.

Q. Have you ever attended a meeting of the Directors of the Western Mutual Benefit Association since it was organized? A. Yes.

Q. Have you ever seen the books purporting to be lists of members? A. I have seen them occasionally. They were open for the instruction of members.

Q. You do not know about its business? A. No.

Q. You have been a Director? A. Yes.

Q. Since it incorporated? A. Yes. We incorporated in May. We did not have a room and have a meeting till the first of May.

Q. You seemed to be in a hurry to send out your circulars; how is this? A. It is perfectly natural for any house doing business to get all the goods and all the material they can.

Colonel Tobin: There is something in that circular that I would like to know about—that is, if Mr. Collins will acknowledge that is the tract issued by the association? A. That is the circular of the association.

Q. Do you know who folded and mailed them—if done by Mr. Brookes, the President? A. I could not tell anything about it.

Q. Is it not the fact that this association, as far as this plan is concerned, has been considerably enlarged since this was issued? A. The plan was modified considerably; the plan we are now working under is different from the first circular issued.

Q. Is not the plan stated in your incorporation in your constitution and by-laws? A. It is.

Q. You say this plan has been changed? A. I think we changed the plan—I think some two months since; not the entire plan, but the mode of assessment—the rate of assessment. There have been other tables added, different somewhat, but all on the assessment plan.

Q. How often have your constitution and by-laws been changed? A. I don't think they have been changed.

Q. You say the plan was embraced in your constitution and by-laws, and you say that it has been changed. Therefore, there has been a change in your constitution and by-laws? A. To conform to this plan, I presume.

Q. How many changes have there been in your organization since established? A. I could not say.

Q. Who have authority to alter or amend the by-laws? A. The Board of Directors.

Q. At any time they please? A. At any regular meeting.

Q. When are their meetings? A. They are on the first Tuesday of each month.

Q. Have you had any general meeting of the members? A. No, sir.

Q. Have your by-laws been printed? A. No, sir; they have not. They are there in copy form for the inspection of any one, in business hours, that wishes to see them—members, or all others interested.

Q. How can the members be informed of a change in your by-laws when they are not printed? [No answer.]

Q. I would ask you: In the form of application for membership and in the certificate, is there not an obligation on the part of members to comply with the laws of your organization? A. Yes.

Q. Those laws have not been printed? A. Have not been printed.

Q. They have been changed by the Board of Directors? A. I won't say positively that they have been changed. An addition is a change, but the circular is not a part of the by-laws.

Q. You say the plan of organization is embraced in the by-laws? A. Yes.

Q. That is the plan? A. Yes.

Q. The one referred to as embraced in the by-laws? A. Yes.

Q. You have changed that plan? A. Yes.

Q. Modified it? A. Yes.

Q. How can members be informed of that change when the by-laws are not printed? A. That I cannot answer.

Q. And still you require members to pledge themselves to obey your laws and constitution? A. I presume that is the idea.

Mr. Spelling: I want to ask you this question, Mr. Collins: Is it not the fact that the officers of the Occidental coöperated with the organizers of the Western Mutual Benefit Association in the organization of the latter? A. Not to my knowledge.

Q. Did not Mr. Riddle send out circulars as the business manager of the Occidental in the interest of the Western Mutual? A. Not to my knowledge.

Q. I will introduce a circular sent out by J. L. Riddle, dated May 1, 1889. Were you a member of the Western Mutual? A. I am.

Q. And a circular sent to one is generally sent to all? A. That is the supposition.

Q. Did you send to Mr. Richard Eaves, of Pomona, California, a member of the Western Mutual, a circular, as follows: "The Occidental Endowment Association having suspended business, five of its members, all of whom are known to be good business men, in order to save themselves, and all others who may wish to join in with them, from loss, and to continue the protection of their relatives in case of death, organize the Western Mutual. Believing it to be to your interest I have reinsured you in this association for the sum of $1,000, the amount you were protected in the Occidental, which policy, together with the paid up certificate for the amount of assessments paid to the Occidental, and the association's terms of reinsurance, are herewith sent for your consideration. The Occidental members are rapidly accepting the reinsurance, and from present appearances a large majority will soon be enrolled. Hoping you will realize that I have done and am doing all in my power to protect you, I am respectfully, J. L. Riddle." On the back of that circular was the following indorsement: "This will answer the question, where has all the money collected gone to." Then follows a statement of the officers of the Occidental, signed by George C. Jones, Secretary; J. L. Riddle, Vice-President of late I. T. E. A. The proposition referred to in that circular of Mr. Riddle I introduce in evidence. Mr. Commissioner, you can examine it, and ask the witness concerning it if you wish. Here is a copy of Mr. Eaves' policy in the Western Mutual, also; and I have another one here that I will offer.

Colonel Tobin: Mr. Collins, that second part I do not understand; the part marked " 2d:" " To all parties in good health, their new certificate will date from the date of the month of his or her coupon." To what does that refer? Does it refer to persons who had coupons in the Occidental? A. I presume it does. This circular was issued while Pollock was President. I had no knowledge of the circular till it was received. I was not President, and have no knowledge. I was not consulted in the issuing of that circular, as Mr. Pollock was then President. I was not President of the Board at that time.

Q. You say a paid up certificate will be issued for the amounts of assessment previously paid. Were the assessments paid to the Occidental? A. It reads that way. Of course I had no knowledge of the issuance of that circular. I was not present at the meeting where that circular was issued.

Mr. Spelling: Mr. Collins, the Commissioner has in his possession a complaint against your association signed by General Jo Hamilton, ex-Attorney-General of the State. It is a very good time to introduce it. It is in regard to Mr. Keener's policy, which I will introduce in evidence.

Colonel Tobin: It is Rudolph Keener.

Mr. Spelling: This is an extract from a letter by General Jo Hamil-

49

ton, Auburn, California, dated August 17, 1889: "It seems from Mr. Keener's explanation, that after the collapse of the Occidental Self-Endowment Association, a new association, calling itself the Western Mutual Association, induced him to send him the policy of the Occidental Self-Endowment Association, promising to send him their policy instead. This he did, sent his policy of one wildcat association and got nothing instead." A. That is from whom?

Q. The proposition made to those members in the Occidental was about this, as I understand it: They were not reinsured, or they were not insured for the amount that they carried in the Occidental, but only the amount of the coupon that was about to become due; was that it? A. No. Our plan calls that they shall join the institution and carry the same amount of insurance in the Mutual that they were carrying in the Occidental; if they were carrying a thousand dollars, they were to carry a thousand dollars.

Q. I think you are mistaken, Mr. Collins. A. That is the idea.

Q. I don't think you understand what the proposition was. [Circular, "To all persons in good health." read.]

Q. We will pass that for the present. What position did you occupy in the Occidental while you were a member of it? A. I was Club Manager at San José.

Q. How many members from first to last did the Occidental have in San José? A. We had ninety-three or ninety-seven.

Q. Were they as a general rule rich people or poor people? A. They were scattered, as you will find in every association.

MR. SPELLING: I want to ask you in regard to Mrs. Pender: Do you know when her coupon fell due? A. I could not tell you now; you have the papers.

Q. Was it ever paid? A. I have no knowledge of it.

Q. Was it not given you to collect six months before the Occidental had collapsed? A. It was given me by Mrs. Pender, because she could not write. I done her a favor to send her coupon into the office for her. That is all.

Q. Is it all the explanation you have to offer about her coupon? A. It was handed into the office, and I am told is still on file. She told me she never got her money.

Q. Did you get a receipt? A. No, sir; I never asked for a receipt; I simply wrote it in her presence—wrote a letter and closed it.

Q. Did she not go to you and demand a receipt? A. Never.

Q. Did you see that coupon any more? A. I was told that it was on file in the central office.

Q. You made inquiry into it? A. Most undoubtedly I did. When I found your letter to me calling for her coupon, I wrote at once, and the answer came that the coupon is on file, and has never been paid.

Q. Did you not undertake the collection of that coupon? A. No, sir.

Q. Did not Mrs. Pender go to you long previous to my letter, and ask you to look after it, and account for it? A. No, sir. How could I account for it?

Q. You were acting as her agent? A. I was not acting as her agent. I done her a favor by writing the letter—as I wrote for all others.

Q. Others got their money, while she did not? A. I don't know.

Q. Did any get their money in that time? A. Lots of them.

Q. Have you had control of her coupon? A. I had no control of it. It was handed to me, and went to the office.

Q. You never paid any more attention at all till I wrote to you on behalf
4—L

of Mrs. Pender—you never reported to her or to me? A. No; I don't consider any one responsible that does a favor for a person—she can't write. The coupon is on file, as I am told.

COLONEL TOBIN: How many members in the Occidental Association in San José? A. I think that the largest amount was ninety-seven.

Q. How many of that amount had coupons paid? A. I don't know. The coupons were not paid to me. The money was sent to members individually; I simply received the money as Club Manager and forwarded it to the home office; received the assessments. Is this investigation according to the subpœna that I got?

MR. SPELLING: It is into associations generally. I want to ask you about other associations in that town. Were you the Club Manager of any other associations? A. No, sir.

Q. Do you know of any other associations that did business in that town? A. I do not.

Q. Don't you know the names of some other associations that did business more or less in San José? A. We have lots of insurance companies there. I am not acquainted only with my own affairs.

Q. Your company, then, seemed to have a monopoly in San José? A. You can call it a monopoly. I don't know the affairs or the doings of other businesses.

MR. SPELLING: I don't know that it is necessary to quote any of these papers, but I will put in evidence another circular issued by the Western Mutual and signed by Morelli, dated May fourth, and that policy of Mr. Eads—he puts in a complaint.

WITNESS: He says that he never received anything in return?

MR. SPELLING: That was Mr. Rudolph Keener, of Auburn.

WITNESS: It seems strange that a gentleman who has not received his policy should not write to the association. He can't be a business man. If I had a complaint to make I would make it right along to the right quarter.

MR. SPELLING: I introduce the complaint of Mrs. Eads against the Western Mutual.

Q. Have many of the poorer classes of people been made victims by the collapse of the Occidental? A. I cannot say in regard to that. If Mr. Spelling wishes to go through the list, I will give him the best explanation that I can. And then it might be my opinion; I might be misjudging the people.

Q. How many members in your new association? A. I am not able at this time to tell.

Q. You understand well the full scope of the association at present? A. There are perhaps some things not fully made plain; but I think I understand in a general way the purpose of the association.

Q. It is an endowment association? A. An assessment endowment association.

Q. Has it a life insurance? A. We have several plans; life or endowment.

Q. Has it any accident insurance scheme? A. You may call it so if you wish. It is partly so.

Q. I want to know if there is anything not embraced—I think you cover the whole field? A. I think so.

Q. I want to find out if there is any plan you have omitted, that you have not tried to take in in your organization? I have one of your leaflets. A. It embraces it all.

Q. It appears to me from this, Mr. Collins, that you have tried to take in every form? A. We have tried to give them the latter forms of insurance, that we consider could be safe—absolutely safe; that has been the intention, nothing else. If there is a better plan in the field I fail to find it.

Q. Your organization is the fourth resurrection, is it not, of the original Texas concern that was founded by Mr. Russell? A. I could not tell.

MR. SPELLING: Five defunct ones.

COLONEL TOBIN: I suppose it is the representative of all those plans?

Q. Has your association levied any assessment? A. The assessments are payable monthly.

Q. Can you approximate the number of members? A. I could not, sir.

Q. Do you know the amount paid in? A. I have no idea.

Q. Do you know when the report is to be issued of your organization? A. I cannot say when the report is called for or not; I don't know whether it is printed; I cannot give you that information.

Q. Can you tell how many members, at the present time, were formerly members of the Occidental? A. No, sir; I cannot.

MR. SPELLING: You are the President of the Western Mutual, and you say you have never examined any of its books, and know nothing of its condition? A. I have looked over the books occasionally; but the monetary matters I don't know anything about; I have made no examination.

COLONEL TOBIN: Who is Treasurer of your organization? A. Mr. Leshir.

Q. Mr. Leshir is Vice-President? A. There has been a change in the officers; there is no Treasurer, because, as yet, there are no funds in hand. We have selected, I think, Wells-Fargo as depositary.

Q. Who elected the officers? A. They were elected at the time of the incorporation.

Q. Has there been any change in the officers? A. I was elected Vice-President, and when Pollock went away I was elected President. Mr. Leshir was Treasurer, and he has been made Vice-President.

MR. SPELLING: Was your organization undertaken for your own profit or for the profit of other people? A. There was no profit in it for several years.

Q. You undertook it out of pure benevolence, and in the interests of other people? A. It was the idea, expecting that in the course of years there would be a reasonable margin of profit. My idea was to get together and to save others and myself if possible.

Q. You have received your coupon in the Occidental, have you not? A. Never received a cent.

Q. Do you know what became of Mr. Pollock—you say that he has gone away? A. I do not.

Q. So you undertook it unselfishly in the interests of other people. Was not Mr. Leshir connected with the Occidental at one time? A. That I could not tell you; never met the gentleman till the time we organized.

Q. Do you know how much money per month, on an average, was collected and forwarded to the Occidental by you as Club Manager? A. I cannot tell.

Q. You can approximate it; say? A. I guess somewhere in the neighborhood of $275 to $300; it would average that.

Q. How long were you Club Manager? A. From its inception:

Q. How long? A. Four years; oh, yes, six years.

Q. What was your compensation as Manager? A. It is laid down in the by-laws.

Q. We have not the by-laws. I don't know if we can get them. I doubt if they have been written out. A. Part of the time 8 cents a member, and part of the time 10 cents a member.

Q. For each month? A. For each month—so much per capita. It is not a very heavy salary.

W. F. HUGHES.

Called as a witness, and sworn.

MR. SPELLING: What is your business, Mr. Hughes? Answer—I am doing a general commission business—real estate and auction business, fire insurance.

Q. Are you acquainted with the operation of mutual assessment and endowment associations in the City of San José? A. I cannot say that I am much acquainted. I have had some acquaintance in the Occidental.

Q. Do you know from the experience and statements of others something about the extent of those operations? A. The extent of those mutual endowment associations?

Q. Yes? A. Yes; I know something about that. I know there are quite a number of them represented in San José, and they have done a great deal of business there. You are talking about these associations generally?

Q. Does the Western Mutual Benefit Association, among others, do business in that city? A. I know nothing, I might say, about the working of that association. I have had circulars from them; was in their office one time, and talked with Mr. Pollock when he was President; and I talked with Mr. Jones, who was the Financial Secretary of the Occidental, and also with Mr. Riddle (very few words with Mr. Riddle) in regard to the Western Mutual.

Q. Did he ask you to join the Western Mutual? A. Yes: he did. I cannot remember the date that I was there, but it was after the date that they moved into their office, No. 10, Flood Building. I was in their office there.

Q. You found Mr. Jones and Mr. Riddle there? A. Yes; and a gentleman whose name has been mentioned here; he is the Secretary, Morelli.

Q. Do you know of any discrimination they made among the members in the Occidental in the proposition that is contained in their circulars? Do you know of any offers to a certain class of Occidental members that were less favorable than those offered to another class of members? A. Well, as to that, I would have to answer simply as my opinion. I should say, and told them so—I told Mr. Jones so at the time I talked to him—that would be a matter of opinion, and no other to verify what I say—I asked Mr. Jones why it was that I, Mr. Levy, and Mr. Leonard, and Mr. Posell, and one or two others had received no circulars; and he explained the matter that it must have been an oversight. I asked him if it was not strange that he should have overlooked so many of those who had been paying so much money into the Occidental—into the original institution—as I understood this was to take the place of the Occidental; and he said to me that it was only an oversight, and desired to give me circulars to take up. I declined the offered proposition, but I took one myself.

Q. Is it not the fact that those who were overlooked in that proposition, or left out, were those whose coupons were about to mature? A. That was the fact.

Q. And those to whom the proposition was made were those whose coupons had a long time to run before they would mature? A. It is a matter of fact, because the coupons of those whose names I mentioned would mature in a very short time; and I put that question to him, if it was not for the purpose of avoiding the responsibility of those whose coupons would mature at an early date; and he remarked that it was an oversight; and I remarked that it was a singular oversight.

Q. And you inferred that those who had created trouble in the old association were those whose coupons were about to mature, according to that circular? A. I don't know about that; I don't know what you mean by creating trouble, unless he meant by asking for loans.

Q. This discrimination? A. I understand, as a matter of course, those who were creating trouble were those who would be wanting their money very soon.

Q. Was the proposition an offer to pay your coupons when they matured in the Occidental, or at a later period than that? A. The proposition made to me was that we must answer for the same amount that we had been carrying in the Occidental, and that at the end of the period when our first coupons would mature in this first organization, we would then receive the coupon due in the Occidental. I asked Mr. Jones how were they going to meet that, if they could not pay the Occidental coupon now; as a business proposition, as a present proposition, how they were to pay both coupons at the end of a fixed term; mine would be about four years, and that was what I think it was in the Occidental.

Q. I will read this proposition: They must become members of the Western Mutual Benefit Association for at least the amount of the coupon allotted them? A. Yes.

Q. The new contract to date from the date of maturity of his or her coupon if you become a member in the Western Mutual? A. Yes; that is correct.

Q. If your coupon matured the first of May, 1889, the certificate in the Western Mutual Benefit Association was dated the first of May, so that that coupon which would have matured in the Occidental did not become due in the Western Mutual Benefit Association until a number of years afterwards? A. Yes.

Q. The new contract to date from date of maturity of his or her coupon was the date of refunding assessments, as specified in the coupon? A. Yes.

Q. Mr. Hughes, as a general proposition in reference to their financial condition, were members in the Occidental and other associations of its kind in San José? A. Their financial condition?

Q. Yes; and their occupations. Speak of that in your own way? A. I am fully convinced that the great majority of them are poor people. I speak from the fact that I had a list of the members of the Occidental in San José; and in looking over that list, my impression is that two thirds of that list were laboring people —people that have very little means—were generally laboring people. There were some exceptions to that.

Q. In some instances, were they not ignorant and credulous people? A. Yes; quite a number of cases were people who were hardly competent to judge for themselves—perhaps a great number of them.

Q. Give the names of endowment or mutual assessment associations that have done business in your town other than the Occidental and Western Mutual Benefit Associations? A. It is very hard for me to remember these names. I know a number of them when I hear them. There was a company who preceded this; that was the same as the Occidental—the Occidental is the successor. There was a company organized in Oakland, the Mutual Benefit Association of— I can't remember.

Q. Who were the officers of it? A. The President of it, T. H. Jordan— W. H. Jordan—he is the head. I took out a policy in that myself at one time and all I paid was the initiation fee. But I am not familiar with the names of these.

Q. Is there one association that Jordan is President of called the Workingmen's Guarantee Fund Association—that is what the mutual endowment association of Oakland is called? A. That is it.

Q. Dr. Smith and Mr. A. M. Thompson were connected with the Self-Endowment Association. Do you know anything about it; did it do some business in your town? A. I could not answer; I remember the name, but I could not say about it.

Q. Did the Pacific Endowment League do some business there? A. Yes.

Q. Has it a membership there now? A. I cannot say.

Q. Do you know who is the collector for it? A. No.

Q. It did business in San José, did it? A. It did business in San José. I had its circulars left in my box frequently, and the agents called on me.

Q. Do you know George Kirber and Ida—Mrs. E. M. Hoeffer? A. I do.

Q. What is the financial condition of these parties? A. Mr. Kirber is in easy circumstances; he is hard working, but he has some property. Mrs. Hoeffer is a poor woman—a very poor woman, and had a hard struggle to pay her assessments. That I know of.

Q. How long did she pay? Can you give the sum total? A. I put it down; she told me what she paid.

Q. Did you get a statement from her signed by her? A. I did.

Mr. Spelling: The statement is as follows: Has paid in $350 the first year; more afterwards. Signed, Mrs. E. M. Hoeffer. A. I don't know exactly how much she paid. She was a member of the Occidental.

Colonel Tobin: Did she get any money in return? A. I would not be positive whether she ever received a loan or not. Her coupon was never paid. Her coupon is due—past due.

[Statement read of Lewis Griepenstruck, George Kirby, witness.]

Q. Are there many more cases similar to this to your knowledge in San José, Mr. Hughes? A. There are quite a number of other cases there in which it has worked a great hardship; I can't remember names. I know there is one woman, a widow, who lived out not a great way from Santa Clara, and who has come down to see me several times; but I am very poor of remembering names.

Q. How much has she paid in? A. She has paid in for about three years. Her policy is about $2,000. She has paid in $350. She was so poor that she could not raise $10 to join in the suit against the Occidental.

Q. Did one of her coupons become due? A. Her coupon was due; and she could not raise $10 to go into the suit; that was the fact.

Q. Do you know of any other instance? A. I could not give names. [Mr. Spelling hands witness a list of names; witness reads.] At least two thirds of these people are poor and laboring. In looking over the list I could mention a number of names, but people object sometimes to having their financial condition exposed.

Mr. Spelling: State in regard to a conversation you had with Mr. Riddle about folding and sending out circulars, about the time of the collapse of the Occidental? A. On Monday—I believe the Occidental was attached either Friday or Saturday, about the twenty-third of March—I could not give dates exactly—on the Monday following I came to San Francisco; went to the office of the Occidental to ascertain the condition of things; did not know that it was attached. Mr. Riddle invited me out, and we had a conversation in reference to the Occidental and its future plans. He stated to me that he had known for a long time that the Occidental could not run. I asked him why, then, professing to be a friend of mine, he did not tell me in October previous, when I had a talk with him, what was its condition. And he said, "I did not dare do it." He said: "If you and everybody else had put your shoulders to the wheel and helped to get new members, we might have gone along." I ,said: "Judge Riddle, I could not conscientiously ask a man to join the Occidental when I felt that it was not on a good financial basis." And he admitted to me then that he had known that it could not run; and he said: "We have got to organize a new institution;" and he says: "To show that I am prepared for this thing, we have a full copy of all the names from the Occidental books; I have had circulars printed and folded and in the envelopes ready to post to each member of the Occidental to whom we think it will be proper that we should apprise them, or those of them who would make desirable members." He says: "There are some Occidental members we don't want, but we are prepared now to send these circulars out." He stated positively that he had been expecting this thing to collapse for months—had known that it could not run.

Q. Did he designate the class of members that were not desirable in the new concern? A. I cannot say that he did, further than that those who were going to press their claims—those whose claims were about due and were about to press their claims—that he did not want them. He asked me to become a Director of this new company.

J. S. AMES.

COLONEL TOBIN: What is your name? Answer—J. S. Ames.

Q. Where do you reside? A. Santa Rosa.

Q. What is your occupation? A. Carpenter.

Q. You are not a capitalist? A. No, sir.

Q. To what extent did you invest in the Occidental Mutual Benefit Association? A. Well, about between $1,400 and $1,600, sir.

Q. Did you accept the propositions made by the Western Mutual Benefit Association, or did they make any to you? A. They made propositions to me.

Q. Were you a member of the Occidental Endowment Association? A. I was.

MR. SPELLING: Do you know what proposition the Western Mutual Benefit Association made to you? A. I did not join any but the Occidental.

Q. Was any proposition made to you after the collapse of the Occidental, taking it for granted that it did collapse, by any other association? A. Mr. Ridley wrote me a letter, he would like me to join the other.

Q. What was the name—the Western Mutual Benefit Association, was that it? A. I think so.

Q. To what extent did you invest in the Occidental? A. Between $1,400 and $1,600.

Q. How much were you insured for in that association? A. My wife and I were insured in all for $20,000—$10,000 each.

Q. For how many years did you continue to pay assessments? A. Paid assessments for about four and one half years.

Q. The sum total paid in by you for yourself and wife amounted to how much? A. In the neighborhood of $1,400 to $1,600.

Q. Did any of your coupons mature? A. One.

Q. How much was the amount of that coupon? A. One thousand dollars.

Q. Did you get that amount when it became due? A. I did not get anything—not a cent.

Q. Did you ever talk to the Directors about your interest in the Occidental? A. I did.

Q. What Directors? A. Dr. Smith, A. P. Overton, T. J. Brookes—that is what I call him—it may have been Brook.

Q. What is Mr. Overton's occupation—is he not a President of a bank? A. I think so, sir.

Q. A railroad builder? A. I do not know about the railroad.

Q. Is he not building a railroad to Sebastopol? A. I do not know.

Q. You say you talked with those men, tell us what they said? A. They told me to stick to it, and when my coupons became due I would get the amount due.

Q. What policies were you carrying? A. Four. Two of my own and two of my wife.

Q. For $10,000 each? A. Each.

Q. You were insured first in the Santa Rosa? A. Last in the Santa Rosa. First in the old office—the Texas Endowment Association. They made it all over in one some way.

Q. Did you make any complaint to these Directors about the non-payment of your coupons, and the refusal or failure to make loans to you? A. Yes; whenever I saw them I did. I did not complain very much. I am not one of that kind.

Q. When were those complaints made? A. Right along for the last year or two.

COLONEL TOBIN: Did you make any attempt to recover what was due to you through proceedings at law? A. I did not.

MR. SPELLING: Tell the substance of the reply you received from Overton, Dr. Smith, and Mr. Brookes. Did you talk to Mr. Carruthers any? A. I did.

Q. Tell in your own way what reply they made, if any? A. They all told me it would be all right. Mr. Carruthers told me if he was me he would drop part of it; he had not much faith in it.

Q. Did he give any reasons for his lack of confidence? A. No.

Q. Where does he reside? A. He resides at Santa Rosa.

Q. What positions did they occupy in the Santa Rosa Self-Endowment Association? A. They were Directors.

Q. What position did Brookes occupy, also? A. Brookes, I believe, was President.

Q. What position did Mr. Overton occupy; simply a Director? A. I think so.

Q. Did Smith occupy any position besides being a Director? A. I don't know.

Q. Was he not medical examiner? A. He was; he examined me.

Q. All but Carruthers told you that it was a safe thing for a year or two before it collapsed? A. They told that to me right up to the time it collapsed—to not more than two or three weeks before.

Q. What is the financial condition of these men, speaking in a general way? A. I wish I was as well off as either of them.

Q. Do you know of any poor laboring men or widow women in the town of Santa Rosa who have suffered from this or any other of the mutual endowment kind? A. I know of some in Santa Rosa, and outside of it I am not acquainted much.

Colonel Tobin: Are you a member of any endowment association at the present time, Mr. Ames? A. I do not belong to any of them; it is the only one I belonged to.

Q. Was any money given to you as a loan from that association? A. No, sir.

Q. And you absolutely lost all you paid in? A. Yes, sir; every cent.

JOHN F. SMITH.

Colonel Tobin: What is your full name, Mr. Smith? Answer—John F. Smith.

Q. Mr. Smith, where are you from? A. From Santa Rosa, sir.

Q. You were a member of the Occidental? A. Yes, sir. My wife was insured in the Occidental.

Q. You were not yourself? A. No; it was my wife, but I always paid it, and attended to it.

Mr. Spelling: Do you know of any other members in Santa Rosa? A. Yes; of quite a number.

Q. Do you know Mrs. Elizabeth Willoughby, who resides down not far from the McNear Hotel, on Fourth Street? A. No, sir; never heard of her; don't know her. I know Mrs. Bennett, a lady who had two policies in this company; her husband had one and she had one.

Q. What was her financial condition? A. Her financial condition was very low. She kept paying, all the time expecting to get paid when the coupon became due. The coupon became due and was not paid. I have the facts of the matter here; a gentleman gave it to me because he could not come, and I brought it down with me; he asked me to bring it down here.

[Statement put in evidence.]

Witness: Now, Mr. Spelling, if you will let me make a statement.

Mr. Spelling: Go ahead. Proceed, Mr. Smith.

Witness: I took out a policy, November 24, 1885, and paid on that policy regularly every month up to 1888, when they commenced to assess double. I used to pay $10 a month; in 1886 and 1887 it was $10 a month, and March 2, 1887, I paid $20 double assessments. Then along from that time up to 1889 I paid $20 a month. We had an insurance of $10,000, and always paid regularly and promptly; but when I took this insurance out first, they told me that in six months I would get $200, and that this would keep the payments up. I thought it was a pretty good thing; but I never got a cent. I went to them, however, a great many times and tried to get money, but they were always embarrassed—could not pay anything.

Q. Did you talk to those Directors? A. I talked to Mr. Brookes, to Judge Overton, and I talked to Mr. Riddle, and they always gave me to understand that the thing was on a good sound basis. All I had to do was to pay my money, and when the coupon became due I would get my money back. But the Financial Secretary, Mr. Wood, when I went to him to get a payment on the coupon, he said that it was impossible; that he could not pay; that in three months he would pay. He told me it was a business office; in three or four months more he would pay. I had so much money insured I had to give it up. I paid in $680.

Q. To cover that policy? A. Up to the smash, I had paid up to March $680. I had paid $700 when they bursted, but I got $20 returned.

Q. Was the coupon due at that time? A. The coupon would mature on the eighteenth of November.

Q. They collapsed in March? A. Yes, sir; but they always told me that the thing was straight.

Q. Was there any effort to get you to join the Western Mutual? A. Yes, sir; after they collapsed I received a letter and went to the office in the Flood building, and Mr. Riddle told me that if I would join that I would in six months get one third of my money, and in another six months get another third.

Q. Did you join? A. No.

Q. Why? A. I did not have any confidence in the people.

Q. Did you recognize most of the old hands in the Occidental? A. They were all there, I guess, mostly. Mr. Riddle said he was there only to help them out. I guess he was the Prime Minister of the whole thing.

Q. Then you thought it better not to throw good money after bad? A. I thought so.

Q. Were you not required to give up your Occidental policy? A. He said all of us that would execute a bond to them, they would see that they got their money back.

Q. Did you talk with Brookes? A. He said he thought that the Western Mutual was a good thing; he was going to join it himself, and was the only way to get our money back. I could not see it that way, and I did not join.

Q. What members of the Occidental do you know in Santa Rosa? A. I know Mr. Peck.

Q. What is Peck's financial condition? A. He works for a living every day. I know Mr. Kewy; he lives close to my house; he works every day.

Q. Do you not know some widows and poor men in this institution? A. There was one woman came to my house. I told the woman that it was very foolish to be worrying about it—that it was as safe as if in the bank; I thought so myself. I believe she got $500; her son is, I think, a lawyer.

Q. That probably accounts for it? A. I don't remember her name. She came to my house, and I told her I thought the money was as safe as in the bank, as I had every confidence in the men who told me so, Mr. Brookes and Mr. Overton.

Q. Did they tell you that it was as safe as in the bank? A. I told that lady so. Mr. Brookes told me that it was perfectly safe; that everything was straight and square.

Colonel Tobin: Did Mr. Overton tell you that? A. I spoke to Mr. Overton a long time ago, and he told me everything was all right.

Q. Is not Mr. Overton a banker in Santa Rosa? A. He is President of the savings bank.

Q. Is he not building a railroad to Sebastopol—helping to do it; one of the Directors? A. I don't know whether he is interested in it or not. He is always interested in anything Mr. Donahue is undertaking.

Q. He has to do with the management and control of railroads in that county? A. I think he has; I would not be positive.

Q. Don't you know he is one of the Directors—a builder of the Sebastopol road? A. I heard.

Q. What is Mr. Brookes? A. He is a farmer in San Joaquin County.

Q. Does he work on his farm? A. He has some one working on it for him.

Q. Is he a poor man or a rich man? A. He is not a poor man. He lives on his farm.

Q. What position does he occupy in Santa Rosa? A. I think he is one of the Directors of the Southern Pacific Methodist College, or Pacific Methodist College.

Q. Don't you know Mrs. Elizabeth Willoughby, that lives across the street? A. I know her boy, but I don't know her.

COLONEL TOBIN read the sworn statement of Mrs. Elizabeth Wilson, September 20, 1889.

COLONEL TOBIN: We have a large amount of correspondence from different parts of the State of the same character.

A. W. BISHOP.

COLONEL TOBIN: What is your full name? Answer—A. W. Bishop.

Q. You are Secretary of the Mutual Endowment of Oakland? A. Yes.

Q. The Mutual Endowment has been in existence five years? A. Since August 7, 1884.

Q. Yours is an incorporated society? A. Yes.

Q. Your plan, besides endowment, is also sick and relief? A. There is both life and endowment—separate and distinct from each other—and the only relief feature is that when members are disabled through sickness or accident, we loan them $2 on each $1,000 on the face of their policy for a period not exceeding eight weeks in any one year, to tide them over any disability, so that they would not lose their membership from being disabled.

Q. Have the rates of endowment been increased since the date of your incorporation? A. They have been increased very materially.

Q. To what extent? A. Well, about 50 per cent.

Q. What was the cause of the change in the rates? A. We found that the rates we adopted first would not meet the liabilities, and therefore they were increased.

Q. How long after the date when this organization was started was this change made? A. About a year and a half.

Q. Then the new plan has been in existence about three and a half years? A. Yes, sir.

Q. Tell what was the rate of assessment on $1,000, say an average age of forty at first? A. It was 90 cents.

Q. What is it at the present time? A. It is $1 20. •

Q. Do you consider anything under $1 20 to be a safe form of assessment? A. I do not.

Q. Do you believe that any endowment association, assessing its members only $1 or under, where the coupon would mature in five years, would be a safe plan? A. No, sir; I don't think it would. I am speaking of course on a basis of $1,000 now. I don't think it would be safe.

Q. How many members had you who were entitled to coupons under the old plan? A. Well, it was about two hundred at the time.

Q. Have the coupons of these two hundred about matured? A. Some of these; most of them, that are still members, they will mature—well, some of them will extend into next year.

Q. About how much would a member under the present system pay into your organization in seven years when the coupons mature—seven years is your limit? A. Seven years at forty?

Q. Seven years at forty, I am speaking of that? A. I stated that hastily, and I may be mistaken. [Looks at card.]

Q. This will be a coupon that will be due in a period of seven years of

$1,000? A. We pay in the association $105 30, and get $200. The $1,000 would extend through a period of thirty-five years.

Q. $105 30 in seven years would get $200? A. He is paying on the same amount through a period of thirty-five years—of course it would be less; of course the interest for the thirty-five years would make his payments for the last years necessarily smaller than the first; but multiplying that by five would give the total amount that he would pay in during the thirty-five years. It would take thirty-five years for him to get the full $1,000.

Q. You say that there are about two hundred members on the old plan entitled to coupons? A. Yes.

Q. About what was the average length of coupons at that time on the old plan? A. They were the same, excepting from the ages of fifty to fifty-five the period was decreased down to four years. We took them in up to sixty; but after fifty-five, under the old plan, one coupon was canceled, if they were fifty-nine; two coupons above fifty-nine; but under the new plan there is no coupon matures in less than five years, and no member is admitted at the age of over fifty-five years.

Q. Was not the old plan more beneficial or advantageous to members than the new plan? A. Oh, materially so. It was disadvantageous to the association as an association.

Q. Now, Mr. Bishop, was the reason for your making the change in your assessment plan founded on the fact that you saw that you could not carry out your contract with your shareholders on the original plan? A. That was the cause of changing.

Q. Or your concern be destroyed if continued on the original plan? A. No doubt of it.

Q. Under your system have you been able to meet all demands? A. Every payment has been met the day it was due, and we have $50,000 in our reserve fund.

Q. I would ask you by way of comparison: Does your association charge a much higher rate of assessment than any other endowment associations? A. I think our charges are the highest of the kind of any association doing business on this coast. I would like in addition to add to that, to state while it is fresh in my mind: In addition to the endowment, our life rates are nearly equal to the old line companies. They are the same as the Fidelity of Pennsylvania—it is an incorporated organization, that is, a mutual company, but incorporated under the laws of Pennsylvania, but that is considered what they call the old line companies—their rates are the same as ours. I took the assessment rate of the New York Mutual Reserve.

Q. Have you had experience in mutual assessment insurance? A. Well, more or less for the past ten years.

Q. Would you explain it to us how it is that a person paying $105 30 into your organization during seven years would be able to get $200 at the end of that period? A. It is on the principle that has been found to be correct in all insurance companies and associations—not only old line, but mutual and coöperative associations—that there is an average in the whole case of 20 per cent of lapses each year; and that lapse is in fact the basis of the accumulation of many millions of dollars which the big companies have now as their surplus—it is from lapses. Taking for instance the Pacific Mutual, they have on their books, I think, some twenty thousand names of members who have joined it, have continued their membership through different periods of time, and I think they are carrying now as persons whose policies are still in force, some four or five thousand. That shows the number of lapses that will occur in all insurance companies and associations. They pay their money in and through some cause or other quit.

Q. What other foundation do you depend upon besides this? A. The other is the interest upon the amount of money that is paid in through the period of time before the member's endowment becomes due. These two accumulations are the only basis upon which you can reduce the actual amount.

Q. Don't you depend upon the influx of new blood, upon the receipts of new members coming in? A. You have got to keep your membership good; but if you depend upon nothing more—if you depend upon the increase of membership to pay the amounts due old members, eventually then you would fail.

Q. What disposition do you make of the funds of your association in order to make interest? A. It is loaned upon real estate.

Q. Anything on loans? A. Our by-laws prohibit the loans of money on anything but real estate, and State, county, or government bonds, with the exception, as I have said before, of the small amounts that we loan to members when they are disabled, in order to tide over their difficulty; that is, a loan upon which they pay 7 per cent interest.

Q. Does your loan vary? A. From five to ten years.

Q. According to the age of members upon entrance? A. Yes.

Q. How many funds have you in your incorporation? A. Three. The general fund or expense fund. The second, coupon indemnity fund, which is the fund for the payment of coupons maturing, either by death or by expiration of time; and the reserve fund, which is not to be less than $50,000, which we have now fully paid in.

Q. How often are financial reports published? A. Semi-annually.

Q. Are they printed? A. Yes.

Q. Are they distributed? A. Yes; distributed to every member.

Q. Do these reports contain full details of the receipts and disbursements of each fund? A. It does in detail of the coupon indemnity fund and of the reserve fund, but not of the general fund—not in detail.

Q. How is it that you do not detail in the publication of the expense or general fund? A. Well, there is no reason, except that to publish it in detail would require a very large space of the papers.

Q. I notice in all the fraternal organizations they publish in detail the receipts and disbursements of the expense fund; why should it not be done by an association such as yours? A. I don't know but that it would be good policy to do so.

Q. Are the moneys paid out by yourself, as Secretary, or are they paid out by warrant on the treasury? A. Every dollar paid out of any description of fund is on warrant, and not upon anything else.

Q. For each warrant paid out, have you the date and name and address stated in the warrant? A. Yes.

Q. But no reports of your disbursements have ever been published? A. None, excepting the general amounts.

Q. By whom can your by-laws be altered or amended? A. At the annual meeting of the members of the association, by a majority vote, or by a two-thirds vote of the Board of Directors.

Q. At any stated time in the interim between the meetings of the association? A. Only at regular meetings.

Q. If a change is made in any of the by-laws, is that change published and sent to all the members? A. Yes.

Q. Are your books open to members? A. Any member has the right to inspect the books at any time.

Q. Would you think it a good thing to place associations such as yours under supervision? A. I think it would. We had a bill last session placing under supervision all associations of every description of life or accident, and also that they should not do business without a surplus of $50,000.

Q. Did you see the bill introduced by Mr. Wadsworth? A. I was there at the time. Our bill proposed to make the reserve fund $50,000, which was provided by our by-laws. It was cut down to $25,000 to accommodate some other associations of this character.

Q. Who introduced your bill? A. It was introduced in the Senate by Mr.—I forgot his name. There were four or five bills drawn, and we met together—we had a meeting of the parties interested in this matter—and they were consigned in the one bill. Our bill virtually was adopted, with the exception of the amount of the reserve fund. Mr. Wadsworth's bill was embraced in ours, with the exception of the reserve fund and some little alterations that Mr. Wadsworth consented to.

J. H. LEONARD,

•Of San José.

MR. SPELLING: What position do you occupy? Answer—City Treasurer and Collector of San José.

Q. Have you been investing in the Self-Endowment Association? A. Yes.

Q. Are you acquainted with the financial condition of the class of people who have invested in such associations in that town? A. Not particularly; only in a general way.

Q. Well, in a general way, what class have invested in these associations; are they working people, or wealthy people? A. The majority are working people; people of the poorer class.

Q. What proportion of these are poor people that work for their daily living—two thirds, three fourths? A. I could not say that; but the majority are working for their daily living for their support.

Q. Do you know what associations have done business in San José? A. I don't know—there are a great many of them.

Q. Do you know the Western Mutual? A. I know of it; I know Mr. Collins well.

Q. Did you have any conversation with the President of the Western Mutual before it was organized? A. I did before it was organized, and at the time it was organized. I was then a member of the Occidental that had suspended, and Mr. Collins was an old friend and Club Manager, and also acted as a deputy of the managers in examining the organization of the Occidental.

Q. Tell what the conversation was? A. At the time of the collapse of the Occidental I saw him and asked him what was to be done. He said he should come to the city to consult with other members and consider what arrangements could be made to protect the old members of the Occidental. On his return in two, three, or four days, he said they had not fully completed their arrangements. I said mine would mature in August of this year, and he said I probably would not get any pay for a year. I called on him after his second visit to the city. He seemed disinclined to talk, and learning my coupon would mature during the year said nothing would be paid to me; that they could not receive me as a member; that they only took in those whose coupons had matured afterward.

Q. Whose coupons had a considerable time to run? A. Yes, sir; that was the idea.

Q. Did he say anything to you as to the source from whence they obtained for him the list of names? A. He did not.

Q. Did you have any conversation with any officer or any Director of the Occidental in regard to that? A. I did not. I had previously expressed dissatisfaction with the management and some of the reports, and Mr. Collins, after his visit to the city and examination of the books, stated that the books were well kept; wished that I could see them; that their affairs were entirely honest, and were flourishing and would succeed.

Q. That is, of the Occidental? A. That is, the Occidental.

Q. How much did you pay in? A. About $325.

Q. How much did you receive? A. I received nothing.

Q. Your coupon did not mature? A. Did not mature. It was to have matured in August, 1889; last August.

Q. From your experience what class of persons were the majority of the members? Were they wage earners, people dependent on their daily labor? A. They were, the majority of them.

Q. Was it while the Occidental was running that you had the conversation with Mr. Collins? A. It was just after it had suspended, immediately after.

Q. Did you not have a conversation with Mr. Riddle before that? A. No, sir.

Q. Did he not tell you the list of members out of which they were going to form the Western Mutual? A. No, sir.

Q. Have you joined the new organization? A. I have not.

Q. Why? A. I have no confidence in it; and, as I understand it, they would not accept me as a member.

Q. Do you know of any instances of poor people who have invested? A. I know these people well. [Looking at list.] I know Mrs. Sechtano and Mrs. Joseph Ingram; I know them both.

COLONEL TOBIN: This is a widow with a large family of children? A. Yes, sir.

Q. Insured for $2,000? A. That was the amount of her first coupon.

Q. How much did she pay? A. She paid over $700.

Q. Paid over $700, and got nothing? A. Yes.

Q. This is signed by Annie Sechtano? A. Yes, sir.

Q. This is another, from Mrs. Joseph Ingham, also a widow lady dependent upon her labor for her support; conducts a small lodging house; joined the Western Mutual Benefit Association of America, Pacific Coast department; she paid all assessments until the society failed in March last; she was to receive $1,000 at the end of the four years, and got nothing? A. She deprived herself, as she told me personally, of the necessaries of life to do that. She paid in about $350—deprived herself of the necessaries of life to do that.

Q. Is there anything else? A. There is a change of by-laws; the old company, without any consultation, entirely changed the plan.

Q. Changed the terms of the contract? A. Changed the terms of the contract.

Q. Made them one sided against the members, when they were already one sided in their favor? A. Yes.

Mrs. E. A. Ainslie.

Mr. Spelling: Where do you reside? Answer—No. 202 Stockton Street.

Q. Were you solicited to become a member of the Western Mutual Benefit Association, of San Francisco? A. Yes, sir.

Q. Who solicited you to join? A. Mr. Riddle, and Mrs. Riddle, and Mrs. Jones.

Q. You talked to Mr. Brookes about it? A. Yes, sir.

Q. Where did you see Mr. Brookes, the President? A. In the Occidental Endowment Association.

Q. Did you see him any time in room 10, Flood building? A. I did; and had a conversation with him.

Q. Did any one hand you one of these circulars? A. Yes; and that was sent to me by mail.

Q. Did the President of the association, Mr. Brookes, hand you one? A. No, sir; he did not.

Q. Did you not see him folding them, and sending them away? A. He was there folding them, and so was Mrs. Riddle. He said he was going into it, and that it was a good thing for him to go into.

Q. Did you say that he had them printed? A. It was a mutual agreement between them all to have them printed.

Q. And Mr. Brookes was folding and sending them out? A. Mr. Brookes, Mr. Riddle, Mrs. Riddle, and Mrs. Morelli were all there folding them and sending them out.

Q. What is your occupation? A. I am a sick nurse.

Q. How much money did you pay into the Occidental Self-Endowment? A. I paid in $600 or $700. I paid them $40 after they were seized, not knowing they were seized; they took it.

Q. And kept it? A. They kept it. After they were seized they took $40 from me.

Q. From whom did you demand it? A. From Mr. Jones and Mr. Riddle.

Q. What position did they occupy? A. Jones was Secretary, Riddle was President.

Colonel Tobin: Are they in the city now? A. Yes; Mr. Riddle is there now, and Mr. Jones is doing the work.

Q. Were you aware that the institution had collapsed at the time that you paid the money? A. No, sir; I had no idea.

Q. To whom did you pay it there? A. I paid it to Riddle's son. I went in with my book that they gave me, and paid my two assessments.

Q. Was the concern at that time in the hands of the Receiver? A. No; but it had been seized.

Q. It had been seized by the Sheriff? A. I was going up the street a few days after, and a lady inquired of me how much money I had lost in the Occidental. I told her I had got a paper that day telling me the concern was prospering. I told her she was mistaken. I went down there; the Sheriff was in there. I had that paper; the "Co-Mutual Alliance," I think, is the paper that they published. It said that it is in a prosperous state. I felt myself quite mortified. I thought I would soon get my $2,000. I have any amount of papers. They sent me one every month.

Q. Do you belong to this Western Mutual? A. No, sir.

Q. Do you belong to any endowment association? A. I belong to the Fraternal, and I belong to the Pacific Endowment. I am one of the first members of the Pacific Endowment.

Mr. Spelling: You never got your coupon paid? A. Oh, no. My

coupon is due. I have got the coupon yet. I never got a cent out of it. I never had a loan. After Riddle, nobody ever got anything; before that they loaned. He got everything himself.

Q. Did you have a conversation with those parties at the time of the Sheriff's sale? A. I was in there. They told me everything would be all right, and to keep quiet.

Q. Who were to make it all right after the Sheriff's sale? A. That is more than I could tell you.

Q. Do you know who was there to bid in those books? A. I don't know. I did not go to the sale at all.

Q. Do you know who gave up the books and papers to be levied on under that attachment? A. I think they were seized before the new Judge. I think they took a list of the members' names while the Sheriff was in the office. I was in there part of the time, and all the clerks seemed to be busy; and I had an idea that they were taking the members' names; and they sent out that way—get them into this new one, and get their money. I told them they had got all I wanted out of me.

J. J. Schneider,

Of San Rafael.

Mr. Spelling: Do you know anything about the business of mutual benefit associations in your town? Answer—Yes; I was a member and Club Manager of the Occidental.

Q. Did you ever take out a policy in the Western Mutual Benefit Association? A. I never did; but a policy was given to me by a solicitor who came to my place. I had some communications by mail in relation thereto; but later on a solicitor came, who was kind enough to bring me out a policy with my name in, so I think it was not quite right. I had the policy with the stipulation that I was to assign any and all of my interest in the Occidental.

Q. Were you required to give up your Occidental papers before you got into the Western Mutual? A. I did not read that; I had no confidence in it; I have it still in my box.

Q. Who solicited you? A. I don't know who the young man is. I supposed it to be Jones; but he was too young to be Jones.

Q. Did any one send you a circular? A. I had several previous, that had come from the main office. Here is one from Riddle.

Colonel Tobin: How much did you pay into the Occidental while you were a member? A. I think over $400. My assessment per month was $3 80.

Q. Did any coupon become due? A. No; the first would be due next March.

Q. Did you ever receive anything? A. It collapsed last March.

Q. It collapsed before the first coupon became due? A. Yes.

Q. Do you know of any more in San Rafael who were in the same boat as you? A. There were some fourteen. We started as a club of twenty-four. I was never in the Western Mutual. They sent me circulars. I had been long a resident, and raised a large family, and felt I could not conscientiously ask people to enter.

Q. Were those of the working class? A. In our club they were not. They were men not possessed of capital, but they had some exceptions.

Q. And who would feel the loss of the capital that they had paid in? A. I suppose one half of them would feel the loss.

Q. Do you know S. S. Barstow, marine surveyor? A. Yes, sir.

Q. Is he a respectable gentlemen? A. Yes, sir.

MR. SPELLING: I have a statement from S. S. Barstow. [Statement read.] A. That is about why they all paid in. The reason why they published, as the lady stated, a paper called the "Co-Mutual Alliance," a paper that gave a monetary statement every month. They did it up to the end of the last month. That letter would be, without question, indorsed by all the members of the club.

Q. The letter that he sent? A. Yes, sir; those are the sentiments of the club consisting of fourteen members—there were twenty-five when they started.

COLONEL TOBIN: There are about two hundred letters of this character.

WITNESS: The association started within two days from the time of this coupon, and they had a method that I would like to make a statement of. They had a method; they seemed to send fair communications to every one all along, until coupons like this became due; the holder was the first one to receive a letter that gave the true financial status of the company, wherein they stated the financial status of the company, and said that he can get within ninety days a certain amount—I think about one third of what is due him; and it appeared to me that they have been doing this kind of business all along, paying about one third, and taking the member's receipt for the whole amount, and thereby published as having paid a certain coupon of $1,000, whereas the fact is that they paid one third or whatever else they could settle for.

Q. It was given here that a lady was offered $15 65 if she gave a receipt in full for $500? A. I inferred that from the character of the communication they sent me.

Q. And not only that, but it was in writing by the Secretary that was in their association. Then they would advertise this coupon paid to her in full? A. It must have been the method of their operations, because they published that paper up to the last. I was looking for one paper. I came down in order to show the character of their statements.

MR. SPELLING: They published one in March, after they were seized? A. I think I have one in my possession after that time.

ROBERT BRUCE.

MR. SPELLING: Where do you reside? Answer—Vallejo.

Q. What business are you engaged in? A. Grocery business at present.

Q. Are you acquainted with the operations of the Western Mutual Benefit Association and its predecessors in the endowment and mutual assessment? A. Not the Western Mutual. I am more or less acquainted with its predecessors, but not much with it.

Q. What predecessors do you speak of? A. The Occidental and the Pacific Coast branch of the Texas—I don't know what you call it. I took out a policy. It is one of those things that a man will do sometimes that he will not do before or after. I paid my assessments, and paid no more attention to it until the Sheriff was put into possession. I never had any faith in it. I insured my wife as well as myself. I was in for six years, and this year both our coupons would become due, and I paid up until the time it failed—I think it was March.

COLONEL TOBIN: How much were you insured for? A. $5,000, paid by coupons, one every six months.

Q. $5,000 for yourself and a like amount for your wife—$10,000 altogether? A. Yes, sir.

Q. Then you would be entitled to $2,000 for yourself and your wife? A. Yes, sir. I paid in between $700 and $800.

Q. How much did you receive? A. Nothing. Never expected it. Was not fooled about it.

MR. SPELLING: How many people in your town, giving a general idea, were investing in that company? A. I do not know. There were a great number invested. Some got their $1,000, and got their portions of it and got out.

Q. The Club Managers got their share? A. I don't know that.

Q. Did one of the Directors live in your town? A. Yes; Dean Harrier.

Q. Did he get his coupon paid? A. He got his coupon paid, but whether in full or not I do not know. I know a Miss McNear that keeps a small millinery shop; she got $600, and the mail before that she got $2,000.

Q. How was she able to get any? A. Her coupon was long due. She got it last fall and her coupon was six months overdue.

Q. Was she not about to sue them? A. I don't know; I think not.

Q. What class of people, as a rule, patronized that institution in your town, poor people or rich people? A. Poor people; fools in general.

Q. Were they not working people? A. Generally your working men has no sense, or women either.

COLONEL TOBIN: You won't find many capitalists going into it? A. Not generally; but I don't blame them, either.

MR. SPELLING: Mary C. Curran—did she sign a statement to be put in evidence here before the Commissioner? A. She did.

Q. Is this the statement? A. Yes, sir.

[Statement handed in in evidence.]

Q. Do you know Mrs. Gillon? A. I do. Mrs. Gillon is in terribly poor circumstances.

[Mrs. Gillon's statement read.]

WITNESS: I know Mrs. Cobbett, that says she has paid in $400 into that institution. She has earned it on the washboard; she has no other means of making a living only washing and ironing.

Q. Do you know Mrs. Sarah Cornell? A. I know her.

Q. What are her circumstances? A. Her circumstances are very poor.

Q. She says she has frequently borrowed money to keep her assessments paid up? A. The distress and feelings of poor women, from paying into the Occidental, no words can express it.

[Statement read of Jorgen Healdsburg.]

MR. SPELLING: I will say now that the Commissioner has a list of three hundred and forty-seven victims of these associations in different parts of the State, and in different companies who have written those letters that we have been speaking of, and have sent their proofs of broken contracts, which proofs are in evidence. We have a list of names here—we will not call them all—the number is three hundred and forty-seven. Those persons, I will say, according to those statements and the evidence contained in their contracts, have paid from $200 to $800 each, and most of them got nothing in return—a few of them getting small loans.

68

C. A. Sawtelle.

Question—Where do you reside? What is your occupation? Answer—Bookseller and stationer.

Q. Do you know anything about the Western Mutual Benefit Association? A. I know their circulars and so forth. I read all their circulars.

Q. Do you know who organized that and put it on foot? A. It is all in the printed list. You have that all, I believe.

Q. Do you know that certain officers of the Occidental Self-Endowment Association had considerable to do in getting that scheme up, and putting it on foot? A. I think the members had more to do with it than the officers.

Q. Were you not in the city after it was organized—shortly after? A. Yes.

Q. Did you ever talk with the President and Business Manager and Secretary of the Occidental in regard to the organization of the Western Mutual Benefit Association? A. I talked with them after it was incorporated; yes.

Q. Did they tell you that they had assisted and taken part in its organization? A. No; they always claimed that those in the circulars were the only getters-up of it.

Q. About what time, Mr. Sawtelle, did the Occidental quit business? A. You have the dates there. I think it was March or April. I think it was April, or the first of May.

Q. Of this year? A. Yes, sir.

Q. Were you not down here in conference with the Directors of the Occidental about the time that they concluded to give it up? A. I was down at the meeting. I was there at the meeting. I could not tell you what month it was.

Q. Do you know the time of the meeting of the Directors of the Occidental when it was in organization? A. Do I know the time? I could not tell this thing.

Q. Don't you know, Mr. Sawtelle, as a fact, that the dates of the regular meetings were the first Tuesday in each month? A. I do not say that I do; no.

Q. Don't you know that it was at the beginning of April that they held that meeting? A. You know when it was, because I have met you there. You have cause to remember. I cannot tell you the day. But so far as being in conference with them, there was nothing of it. I happened in there to see what was going on.

Q. Did you not hand in your written resignation at the time? A. No; I did not hand in any resignation. I simply declined to accept any appointment as Director.

Q. They were desirous of making you a Director? A. Yes, sir.

Q. At that meeting did they not pass a resolution to have the association carried through as an insolvent, unless they got terms? A. Yes, sir.

Colonel Tobin: Were there many members of that association in Sacramento? A. There were about one hundred and twenty-five in Sacramento; but there had been a great many more than that. There had probably been four hundred or more—in the neighborhood of four hundred.

Q. Do you know of any who were paid their coupons? A. Yes; a great many received the full amount of their coupons, and a great many others received payments as the Board saw that the institution would pay or could pay—share and share alike. A good many got the full amount. Then, when it was figured out that it could not pay every dollar, they cut down the amount to be paid, and a good many got their payments on that figure.

Q. What class of people were generally in it? A. Well, sir, there were all classes; some of our wealthiest men, and some poor people, so far as it goes.

Q. Do you know of any endowment association having headquarters in Sacramento, having regular offices and doing business? A. There are several that have their agents there so far as that goes.

Q. That have their regular agents there? Could you mention any at the present time? A. I don't know as I could.

Q. How long were you a member of the Occidental? A. I guess probably seven years—six or seven years.

Q. Did you receive your coupons? A. Oh, no; I was a nine-year member.

Q. How much did you pay into the association? A. Take it altogether I paid on three policies, the payments on which was $700.

Q. And never got anything for it? A. Nothing at all.

COLONEL TOBIN: What, in your opinion, was the main cause of the failure? A. I think the whole cause was simply a few dissatisfied parties who would not take their pro rata of cash; in other words, that they were not satisfied with a smaller amount than their contract called for. The agreement and contract was to get $1,000 or whatever the profits of the association might be, and they all understood it as $1,000 apiece. A year and three or four months before it suspended they cut down the payments to $1,000, it paying them $2 for every $1 they paid in on assessments, which I think you have sense enough to see is a very fair and square proposition. It was run right over a year on that proposition. Parties brought suit; no money coming in there was nothing to pay out.

Q. Did they not promise more than they could perform? A. In part.

Q. Why did they fail? A. On account of the carelessness of back management. Instead of figuring it they sat down and did not make provision for the future as they ought to have done. They should have increased their assessments to one every fifteen days. They did later on.

Q. Were you the Club Manager at Sacramento? A. Yes.

Q. And your name was published as a Director for two months before the collapse? A. Not quite two months. That is, it was published in leaflets.

Q. Were you present at the general meeting? A. Yes.

Q. At that time you were elected Director? A. I was simply appointed Director, and declined to accept. A Director proposed me; it was moved and seconded. I declined.

Q. Were you the Chairman of a committee last January to report to the association? A. I could not tell you.

Q. As Chairman of the Finance Committee? A. I don't remember; I have been on the Finance Committee three or four times.

Q. Did you make an examination of the books last January? A. I have made an examination of the books, but understand, I did not expert the books. I do not know the date.

MR. SPELLING: Did you receive the "Co-Mutual?" A. Yes.

Q. I see in February, the month before it failed, your name published as a Director? A. I did not see it in the paper; I know it was published in the leaflets. Their publishing my name as Director particularly did not make me so. They cannot make a man a Director unless he accepts it; whether my name is published or not does not make me so; I never was a Director in the association.

COLONEL TOBIN: Don't you think it very necessary that all these associations should be controlled and regulated by law? Don't you think they should be under the Insurance Commissioner or some other State officer? A. Yes, sir; that is my idea, and file a report quarterly or semi-annually, so people can go and know exactly what is what.

Q. You made an examination last January and reported? A. I did. That is, it may have been January or February.

Q. The report was published in the "Alliance?" A. I think they [generally published the report in the "Alliance."

J. CLAYPOLE,
Santa Rosa.

MR. SPELLING: Did you occupy some official position or agency? Answer—I collected some for them, and acted as agent for them.

Q. You were Club Manager for them? A. Yes.

Q. How long? A. About ten months.

Q. How many paid assessments? A. Something between seventy and one hundred.

Q. As a general thing what class of people were they—merchants and bankers, or poor people? A. They were divided. Merchants and bankers and poor men and poor women, and some rich women—all went in for speculation.

Q. To what class did the majority of them belong? A. In Santa Rosa the rich class was in a minority. The majority were common laborers. I made a contract that all accept $2 for $1. Those who did not get $1,000 last year, they made a special contract to take $2 for $1.

Q. Don't you know that Mr. Peck made a special contract, and did not get anything? A. I know it; and why did not he get it? He brought suit. I was in Class A for $500. I lived my coupon out, and the year before it was due the company said they could not possibly pay $3 for $1, and came to me with a written obligation, and asked me if I could not accept $2 for $1. I did, and I got it.

MR. SPELLING: But you know some that did not get it? A. Yes.

Q. And you worked for the company? A. I worked to sell coupons for the company; I worked as an agent; tried to get members of the company, and I got many members. It is a mutual concern, and the cause of it becoming defunct is the fault of the members who have ceased to pay. I made a calculation that if every member had paid his regular assessment without drawing, there would have been no need for any payment of money at two to one; they would have had plenty of money, and gone on to-day. They made a mistake when they loaned money. They have $50,000 loaned out they can do nothing with. I borrowed some of that myself. My wife was not out. She borrowed $100. She got no thousand, but she got that $100. I got, while Club Manager, 10 cents for every assessment paid—not 10 cents on the dollar; it would not pay me $15 a month. I want to tell the facts as I understand them. There are a great many ladies in that institution; some of them very poor. One of these I told: "If every member in that institution, two thousand three hundred, will pay the assessments, there is no trouble in your getting your money." There is not one out of five of those who got his $1,000 that continued to pay assessments; he says: "I am ahead of the company now, and I will quit."

COLONEL TOBIN: Is not that the general rule in other associations? A. That is the general rule in any association where they go in for speculation.

MR. SPELLING: Suppose they all paid and kept paying, where are they to get $2 for $1? A. They can get it easily in the profits of the institution. If we can work and get new members to pay us off, we would get along. We make the profits if a man pays and goes, and others come in his place, and his endowment runs on three or four years along.

Q. Some are bound to pay in a lot of money and lose it in order for others to get their money? A. That is true in all insurance.

Q. Who was your predecessor as Club Manager there? A. Mrs. Mieger. She got her two for one in the written statement. All that got their money agreed to take their 25 per cent.

Q. Do you know of anybody else getting their money except you and. Mrs. Mieger? A. I think there were six or seven.

Q. Six or seven out of one hundred and twenty-five? A. There was not one hundred and twenty-five there.

Adjourned till next day.

———

J. J. VASCONCELLOS.

Called.

Mr. Spelling: What is your name and place of business? Answer—My name is J. J. Vasconcellos; my place of business 524 Washington Street.

Q. Have you any experience as a member of endowment and mutual assessment associations? A. Yes; some.

Q. What association have you been a member of? A. I was a member of the Occidental Self-Endowment Association.

Q. Any other? A. Not an endowment, I don't think.

Q. Well, they may not be in that name, but I mean any life insurance company? A. I belong to an association, policy payable at death.

Q. You were a member of that institution in January last? A. Yes.

Q. Did you take the "Co-Mutual Alliance" at that time? A. Yes.

Q. Mr. Sawtelle has stated that as Chairman of the Finance Committee he made a report in January. Do you remember reading that report? A. I do.

Q. Do you recollect the substance? A. I could not tell the substance. I think the purport was that it was in a better standing than it had been for years. I had the paper that I turned over to you. It was in January or February.

Q. How long after before it closed? A. I closed them out in March.

Colonel Tobin: Why did you close them out? A. I brought suit for my coupon and they would not settle with me.

Mr. Spelling: Did that report of the Finance Committee state that it was founded on an examination into the affairs of the association? A. I think it did.

Q. What time did you square up with them? A. Well, I think I squared up with them, sold them out, on the eighteenth of April.

Q. But you did not get satisfaction in that sale? A. I did not get satisfaction.

Q. You settled with them since? A. No, sir.

Q. Do you know anything about the organization of the Western Mutual Benefit Association? A. No, sir.

Q. Don't you know who organized it? A. If I remember aright, I think after I attached, I don't know whether I am right or not, but some institution of the like name was started by the officers after I closed them out. They started an office in Room 10, Flood building.

Q. Do you know anything about Jones, of the Occidental, going round and buying up lapsed policies? A. Yes; I know where Jones sent round buying proxies for lapsed policies.

Q. And getting powers of attorney? A. Yes.

Q. And drawing money on them? A. Drawing full money; yes, sir.

Q. Who did that business, do you know? A. I know of one in particular; his name, I think, was P. D. Guardmire.

Q. Do you know of an instance in which he did it? A. I know of one only that I have evidence of.

Q. With whom was it transacted? A. That transaction was with W. H. Ryan, of Arroyo Grande.

Q. In this State? A. Yes, sir.

Q. Do you know how much he gave for that lapsed policy? A. All I have is the statement of their paper, purporting to pay him $1,000.

Q. How much was paid? A. None, to him; he did not receive a dollar, although the paper stated he received $1,000.

Q. Do you know who reinstated that policy in that company, so as to put it on the books in the regular order of payment? A. I think it was Mr. Riddle. The policy is signed by T. J. Brookes, as President, with George C. Jones, as Secretary. [Policy here shown to the Commissioner.] That is the coupon that they cut off. I would like to state that that policy was not issued at that date—it was not issued when it purports to be. It claims here that it was issued in 1884, but it was not; that policy was not issued at that date.

COLONEL TOBIN: You state that although this policy here is dated the twenty-fifth day of February, 1884, that it was not issued at that date. At what date was it issued? A. It was issued some time in 1887; I think in May. I will state the purport of this policy: Mr. Ryan was insured in two policies—they were having two policies, A and B. A was an endowment policy; B policy was a death policy. He belonged three or four months to the institution, and when the "Chronicle" came out and smeared it all over, Mr. Ryan gave up. He stopped paying assessments and the policy lapsed. He thought it good for nothing, and he dropped it, and destroyed all the papers he had; and when this Mr. Guardmire went down to him, Mr. Ryan stated to him that he had no policies at all.

Q. Was Mr. Guardmire an agent? A. Yes; Mr. Guardmire purported to be an agent, and was getting powers of attorney with which to make collections on the death of policy holders whose policies had run out, and he wanted Mr. Ryan's power of attorney—that had no policy—which he could get reinstated himself.

Q. Because he had burned them? A. He destroyed them. He had nothing to do with them as a member, except that his name was on the books of the company. They then issued this in lieu of the policy originally issued, because the original policy was destroyed.

Q. This coupon that you have offered to us is dated 1884? A. It bears date of the former policy.

MR. SPELLING: To make it appear straight on the books of that institution? A. He having no policy they had to show that the policy was there in order to take the coupons up. Then they issued this, purporting to be of the same set as the former policy.

Q. Did Mr. Guardmire draw the $1,000? A. I suppose so, sir. He had the power of attorney, and the paper states $1,000 was paid to W. H. Ryan; and instead of that I suppose it was paid to him as his attorney.

Q. You don't know to whom it was paid? A. I don't.

COLONEL TOBIN: But you know Mr. Ryan did not get it? A. No, sir; I know positively Mr. Ryan did not get it.

Q. Do you know, is this a common practice to have men to buy up policies of this kind who are interested in the cashing of coupons? A. I understood so—the buying of lapsed policies.

Q. Who are engaged in this business? A. Generally the officers, with subs., and the heads of the clerks—whoever they can buy to do their dirty work.

Q. Did you make them come to time by attaching them, so far as your claim upon them was concerned? A. No, sir; only so far as I could.

Q. How much was due you at the time of the attachment? A. $1,755.

Q. How much had you paid in at that time? A. Somewhere between $800 and $900 paid in.

Q. By attaching them how much did you recover? A. I recovered three of the coupons—four hundred and twenty odd dollars.

Q. You were the first? A. No, sir; there was an attachment before mine; that was the reason why I was not. I prided myself on being the first, but found I was No. 2.

Mr. Spelling; You heard of a great deal of that kind of speculation in lapsed policies in that institution? A. Yes; I have no evidence in this case. But I have heard of a good deal of that kind of speculation being carried on in that institution since 1887.

Q. Did you ever talk with the President, Mr. Brookes, about it? A. Yes.

Q. Did he ever admit to you that it had been to the extent of $30,000? A. I cannot say that an amount was stated. But he stated that there was crookedness there, and he would have no crookedness while he had the control of it.

Q. Do you know what the financial condition of that institution was at the time Sawtelle made his report as member of the committee? A. Said it was first rate.

Q. What was its real state? A. Not a dollar except as could be cleaned up from its effects.

Q. About its indebtedness—have you an idea of the extent of the indebtedness as it appeared from their subsequent statements? A. No; only as they came out after I made the attachment.

Q. Then what did it say about it? A. They claimed then they were $100,000 behind; $100,000 more behind than they had money for.

Q. Are any of the gentlemen who were prominent in the Occidental connected with these associations at the present time? A. Not to my knowledge except Mr. Riddle. I think Mr. Riddle still carries on an institution, one that has sprung out from that. He was then the Vice-President and Manager of the Occidental.

Q. Do you know what association he is connected with at the present time? A. I do not.

Q. Do you know of any other except Mr. Riddle? A. Mr. Riddle and Mr. Jones were the only ones that I know of. They went out from the Occidental rooms and started this other institution across the way that I don't know the name of.

Q. If the books were properly kept, the Directors and officers were bound to have known the liabilities at the time this report was made up by the Financial Committee, should they not? A. Should have known; yes, sir.

Q. Was that report sent to the members generally? Published in the "Co-Mutual Alliance?" A. I think it was, sir; the purported report.

Q. Is not that where you saw it? A. Yes, sir.

Mrs. Addie L. Miller.

Called.

Mr. Spelling: What is your name? Answer—Addie L. Miller.

Q. Where do you reside? A. In Cloverdale, Sonoma County.

Q. Have you had any experience as a member of the Self-Endowment Association? A. I have.

Q. What is the extent of your dealing with that association? What association was it in the first place? A. It was connected with the Texas.

Q. Was it the Mutual Self-Endowment of America? A. I think so. I have all the papers.

Q. Was it the Occidental? A. It is the Occidental now.

Q. How much money did you pay to it? A. I could not give you the exact figures, but it was in the neighborhood of $500.

Q. Did you ever get anything in return? A. No; only drew out what they called a loan of $100; that was three years ago, I think.

Q. How much did they promise you? A. After two years, I think it was, we were to receive $100 every nine months—I think somewhere in that neighborhood.

Q. Do you know how much the amount of your policy was? A. $5,000.

Q. How much were you to receive as a coupon in that policy? A. $1,000.

Q. How much did you receive? A. $100.

Q. Did you have any trouble, Mrs. Miller, in getting the money to pay those assessments; and if so, tell what it was? A. We did have very much trouble. In the commencement of this business with this institution my husband was able to labor, and had good work in Cloverdale. In two to three years after the time the company run out his business was ruined there, and we had to seek other business. Business run down. We went to Mr. Shaw, the banker there, and he assisted us to pay our assessments. But the last year (we were paying $4 20 every eighteen or twenty days) we had to pay $8 40. The assessments were doubled. We were not, under the circumstances, able to pay without assistance. Mr. Shaw assisted us, and to secure him we mortgaged our home. We have lost our home.

Colonel Tobin: You have lost your home through it? A. In part. There is a little mortgage beside it. If we had drawn our $1,000 it would have straightened everything.

Q. Is your husband a well man now, able to work, or is he an invalid? A. He is not altogether an invalid, but he is getting on in years. He is sixty-eight years old.

Q. Are there many in Cloverdale or around there who have invested money in this institution? A. A good many.

Q. What is their condition? A. Some of them are working people depending on their labor; others are in better circumstances, able to survive it.

Q. Can you tell us the reason they put so much confidence in the Occidental? A. I suppose it was the flattering words of Riddle and wife, who had visited there, went from place to place to procure new members, sent out their circulars, and every month came a paper telling the working order of the company.

Q. Did they not place special confidence in the financial standing of some of the Directors? A. I don't know. It was supported by good Directors. We did, of course.

Q. Did you know some of the Directors? A. I am not acquainted with any of them, except Mr. Riddle and wife.

Q. Do you know of other Directors, except Riddle and wife, who reside in Sonoma County? A. I don't know by personal acquaintance. There is one at Santa Rosa; he is a banker there.

Q. What is his name? A. I cannot call it to mind now.

Q. I have them here in the "Co-Mutual Alliance;" did you receive that? A. We received it most of the time; sometimes we missed copies. I think I have still the last one at home. I have a good many for five years. We paid for it also.

Q. Do you know the names of these Directors? A. They have changed Directors different times since we have been members.

COLONEL TOBIN: Have you been in any other endowment association? A. No; not in this State.

Q. Were you invited to become a member of this Western Mutual Benefit Association, that succeeded the Occidental? A. There was some paper sent, but I took no notice of it. I said: "We don't want it." I felt very discouraged and disheartened—disgusted I might say—with such an institution as we had been supporting.

Q. I understood the paper came from the same source as the Occidental? A. Yes; or they would not have sent it. I learned from Mr. Miller before he left home, that he had been speaking to one of the members, and they told him to get his money back he must join the new association. I think the letter was from Riddle.

Q. Are any other persons here from Cloverdale who are interested in it? A. Not that I have any knowledge. I am glad to give evidence because we have suffered very much.

[MR. SPELLING read specific complaint by General Jo Hamilton.]

WILLIAM CRUSE.

Called.

MR. SPELLING: Where do you reside? Answer—In the city.

Q. Have you had any experience as a member of mutual assessment or endowment associations? A. Yes, sir.

Q. What ones? A. Occidental Self-Endowment.

Q. Have you not been a member of some other? A. No, sir.

Q. How much did you lose in the Occidental? A. Well, I never reckoned up the full amount, but I got the receipts here. I used to pay $5, when I joined it first, every twenty days.

Q. Did they double your assessment? A. Then I used to pay $10 every twenty days.

Q. Did you ever get anything back? A. Not a cent.

Q. Can you give an estimate of what you paid in? A. I think close upon $400.

Q. Are there any special circumstances connected with it that you would wish to relate? A. I don't know of anything, but I don't think these things are of much account for any one to risk his hard won earnings in. I don't see any security either for a man to get his money on. They are the same parties now in the Flood building that were in the Phelan.

COLONEL TOBIN: You never received anything? A. Not a dollar.

Q. Did one of your coupons become due before they failed? A. It would be the next month. I took a policy of $5,000, and I was to receive $1,000 every four years. The first endowment was $100 the first year; then about nine months I would receive $100, and so on till the four years would expire—I would have my $1,000 drawn.

Q. Did you get $100? A. Not at all. I never got $1.
[Mr. Spelling read written testimony of John Flood, Los Angeles.]

C. N. JENKINS.

Called.
Colonel Tobin: What is your name, Mr. Jenkins? Answer—C. N. Jenkins.
Q. Residence? A. Marysville.
Mr. Spelling: Have you been acquainted somewhat with the affairs of life endowment associations in your city? A. I have.
Q. What self-endowment associations have been doing business in Marysville? A. This one that started there, called the Texas Self-Endowment Association, I suppose, is about the one that you have reference to.
Q. You can mention those that have done business there? A. I know that that has done more business than any of the others; half a dozen times more than any of the others.
Q. To what extent has your association been doing business in Marysville? A. The Occidental was quite extensively circulated in Marysville. They had an agent there that labored and got a great many connected with it.
Q. Were there fifty or sixty? A. I should say as many as fifty—perhaps more. I know there were a good many.
Q. Some women, were there not? A. Yes.
Q. Do you know of any cases of special hardship in connection with it? A. I don't know, I may say, but one case in our neighborhood, and that has really been a hardship. It is an old Irishman, who depended on whatever a man told him to be so, and had hard work to get along, and had mortgaged his place to pay assessments. I paid assessments—two or three assessments—rather than let him lose his place; he is going to lose it now. He has mortgaged it to a gentleman there to get money—$600—and now the mortgage has run out; he is Mr. Patrick McCabe. He came to my place yesterday, and he says: "I can tell you nothing more than I know; you all know about my circumstances." I have seen him every week for the last ten or fifteen years. His wife is also sick abed—not able to do anything.
Q. So he had to pay assessments on both and got nothing in return, and they were payable? A. Were payable, and he got nothing in return.
Q. How much had he paid in? A. I don't know. The last time I was talking to him it amounted to about $700; and what he has paid in since I don't know.
Q. How much have you paid in, yourself, Mr. Jenkins—into the Occidental? A. I don't know. I figured it up, but know I got about even in it. I got my first coupon.
Q. You demanded your rights of them? A. Yes.
Colonel Tobin: I want to ask your opinion: You are a representative in one of the fraternal organizations, are you not? A. I am Grand Master of the State of California in the Grand Lodge of Odd Fellows.
Q. I ask your opinion with regard to associations such as the Occidental. Do you consider it to be a coöperative association? A. I can hardly see how it can be. I never should have gone into it myself if it had not been for the—I was not solicited by the agent in Marysville; it was a gentleman who had the handling of it on the start—came here from the city—his name you know, Mr. Spelling—to run this thing in the first place.
Mr. Spelling: S. H. Ward.

PORTION OF INQUIRY RELATING TO SOURCES AND SUFFI-
CIENCY OF REVENUE OF ENDOWMENT SOCIETIES.

E. H. BACON.

Called.

COLONEL TOBIN: What is your name? Answer—E. H. Bacon.

Q. You are the editor of the " Pacific Coast Review?" A. Yes.

MR. SPELLING: Will you briefly give the history of those associations which succeeded each other and finally culminated in the Western Mutual Benefit Association—the one which we are now investigating? A. The Western Mutual I don't know anything about. The first association of that kind established in the world was in Texas—at Long View, Texas—the Mutual Self-Endowment and Benefit Association of America; office at Long View, Texas. Then they established a branch in San Francisco at 7 Powell Street, with a Mr. Russell in charge of it. This was in 1877. They all failed. It was the Pacific Coast branch of the Mutual Self-Endowment of this same association; and about six months before the coupons began to mature in this Texas association it failed. This other branch established a second organization, and very soon after its coupons began to mature it also failed; and then out of it had grown two or three associations, but the real successor was the Occidental. There were three further associations which sprung out of this Pacific Coast branch, but they also failed. The principal one was the Occidental, because it took up the coupons of the Texas branch and assumed obligation for them; and as soon as those coupons began to mature, then the Occidental became embarrassed, and the officers that were in charge of it abandoned it or disposed of it in some way to the officers of the Santa Rosa association. The two associations were amalgamated; and as there were considerable new loans, in that way a collapse was temporarily avoided; but when the coupons began to become due the company failed.

Q. What company was it? A. The Occidental. That has been the history of all endowment associations, and in their nature and plan they must fail as soon as the first coupon begins to mature.

Q. Do you know what membership the Pacific Coast branch of this concern had on this coast? A. I examined the books; they had nearly all poor people—laboring people; 40 per cent of them were servant girls.

COLONEL TOBIN: As far as you know, Mr. Bacon, is it not the fact that the largest percentage of those in this association were women? A. I can't tell. We have complaints from both men and women.

MR. SPELLING: Have you an idea of how many people suffered loss on account of the operations of the Pacific Coast department of the Texas company—you have had an opportunity to ascertain that? A. I should say about one thousand one hundred.

Q. And the Occidental succeeded that, and got up its membership from that company, and got new members—brought in fresh blood? A. Yes.

Q. How long did the Occidental run? A. Dating from the time of the organization of the Pacific Coast branch till when the obligations first matured, I should say that it ran about five years—perhaps less than that.

Q. Do you know what was the maximum membership of the Occidental?
A. No, I don't know anything about it.

Q. You don't know anything about the extent of losses to members in the Occidental? A. Nothing more than that we had complaints from persons who lost from $200 to $300.

Q. Do you know what its obligations were at the time it failed? A. I did know that, but I forgot it.

Q. Was it not $178,000, matured coupons? A. I don't think so much as that.

Q. Was it not $178,000, to mature in 1879? A. I can readily believe it was a much larger sum than that.

Q. And as much more for two or three subsequent years? A. No; it would not be so much more.

COLONEL TOBIN: Give a rough estimate. What was directly due at the time? A. My impression is that it was reported to be about $65,000, and that, of course, does not represent those whose claims were about to mature. There was $60,000 or $70,000 already due; it was a large sum.

MR. SPELLING: I asked you yesterday evening to give an estimate of the future liabilities of the Occidental at the time of its collapse? A. That would depend upon the age of the membership.

Q. Do you remember the amount that would fall due in 1889, according to their own circular that Riddle sent out? A. I don't remember. They did print some figures of what they owed.

Q. I have a circular which shows $178,000 to fall due in 1889, and a still greater sum in 1888.

COLONEL TOBIN: Mr. Bacon, on yesterday you gave us some account of the successive metamorphoses of the Texas concern. Do you remember the year in which the first one of these associations, the Texas concern, started here? A. Started in Texas, I think in 1882 or 1883.

Q. When was it started here? A. In 1883.

Q. Was that the forerunner of the different endowment associations in this State? A. That was the forerunner; brought here by a man named Russell, from Texas—Russell and J. H. Ward. He was a bad egg, too.

Q. This original association then underwent four or five transformations? A. The original association underwent no transformation. It established branches in Kansas and California, and it had a great long list of spurious indorsements of leading men.

Q. Is it not the habit of associations of this character to publish fictitious names as references? A. It is. That I have found out from my own correspondence.

Q. These associations are in the habit of publishing the names of persons as references that they have no permission to use? A. No permission whatever.

Q. Could you give an instance of that character? A. Senator Stanford's name was used by an association in this city, and I received a letter from him, in his own handwriting, stating they were not authorized to use his name, although it was stated that they had received permission from him and others.

COLONEL TOBIN: I would like to call attention to two names in the prospectus of one of these associations—Governor George C. Perkins and Mr. Henry M. Black. I called upon both of these gentlemen myself and asked them whether they had given permission for the use of their names, and they both denied having done so. Mr. Black called upon Mr. Oakley, who is the President of the association, with me, and demanded that his name be removed from that list of references. I only called upon two, and I found just as I stated.

Q. You have had some experience in the same line, in other names besides Mr. Stanford's? A. That is the only one I recollect just now. I received letters from various prominent business men denying having given permission to use their names in connection with the association. The name of Governor Ireton of Texas was also used, especially by the Texas association.

Q. Now, from your observation, do you find that the same men connected with these endowment associations, after one has collapsed become the founders of a new organization? A. Yes. They are identified with these successive ones. They are professional organizers of these associations.

Q. There are some connected with the organizations at present doing business that did belong to old defunct associations? A. Yes; several of them. I don't remember any names now except the Russells, who were the professional organizers that I spoke of. Ward was connected with two or three; I don't know where he is—he has a citation from the States Court. The man who originally established the Bankers' Relief Association of San Francisco was a professional organizer. He established cne in Portland under the same name and sold out for $4,000. It has since failed, and he is not now connected with the San Francisco association. Probably he sold that out also, for he admitted that is his business.

. Q. What is his name? A. I don't recollect it now. I have it at my office.

MR. SPELLING: Who organized the Bankers' Mutual Relief organization? A. They have a new lot of men in there now. I cannot recall his name. R. P. Thomas was President of the association at the time it was first organized here, and the Secretary at that time was the real organizer, and is the party who I am referring to.

COLONEL TOBIN: Then of those who originally organized these endowment associations you know of only two or three connected with the present associations? A. That is all, for the reason that some twenty-five of them have failed, and they don't continue to be in business at the old stand.

Q. What is the average length of life of these associations? A. About one year after the first coupons have matured. None of these associations have survived six years. Of the endowment associations not one of them has survived six years.

MR. SPELLING: What do they do with the first batch of coupons? Do they pay them, or stave them off? A. They are supposed to pay them.

Q. Don't they compromise, or stave them off? A. That depends upon what you call the first coupons. The first coupons are those that mature in the specified fraction of a man's life expectation.

Q. Don't they reap the richest harvest about the year when they pay off a few coupons, and get the leverage of that advertising? A. That generally occurs at the expiration of the fourth year, and then the first coupons gather up, and then they are not able to survive the second year's coupons.

Q. Who generally receive the first year's coupons? A. The oldest man or woman, and not the oldest member. The life expectation of young people is a great deal more than that of the older people, and their coupons fall due in an agreed upon fraction of the life expectation, which leaves, I think, one fifth.

Q. Is it not the fact that the professional organizers generally manage to have the first coupons? A. Yes.

Q. How do they manage then in case they were young men? A. That I cannot tell you.

Q. Would it not be by getting hold of or procuring old men, and by getting their lives on the books, and by dummies? A. Very easily done, and it would almost defy detection; or take a fictitious name and pay the fees on it and hold the coupons themselves and the certificate of membership.

Q. Now, with regard to age, I would like to ask you, Mr. Bacon, since you have had great experience in these matters: Where an association issues only endowment policies to the living, and has no death policy, why would it not do to have intervals of years established without any regard to the member's age on entering; for instance in some of these organizations they have maturity tables, notwithstanding the fact that they issue only endowment policies. No policies paying anything in case of death except the next maturing coupon, now how can the question of age affect the individual in that case? A. It is not involved at all, and it would be considerably easier if it were ignored entirely.

Q. Why is it, then, that they have this maturity table and discriminate between different ages? A. Well, I could not tell.

Q. I have been trying myself, and the only reason I can imagine it is done is to give them an appearance of doing business on the life insurance plan? A. Yes; that is all.

Q. In other words, to give members a belief that they are doing business on an insurance basis? A. And concealing the fact that it is merely a gamble; certainly it is not an insurance.

Q. You stated that none of these organizations have lasted more than five years. Could you give us an idea of the average age of these associations on the coast? A. None of them have survived six years.

Q. What is the average age? A. There is no reason why every one of them shall not survive six years, as that is the time when the coupons mature.

Q. What is the usual period when the coupons mature? A. At the expiration of the fourth year. That represents the agreed upon fraction of the life expectation of the oldest members.

Q. What do you consider would be a safe monthly assessment for $1,000, due and payable at the end of four years, with monthly assessments? A. That depends upon the increase of membership entirely. If they increase fifty a month, they could probably pay the first assessment coupons for about 75 cents a month or less.

Q. Some old line insurance companies have the endowment plan payable at certain intervals? A. Nothing like this.

Q. I want you to explain the difference between the plan of the old line insurance and the modern endowment? A. The old line system is a definite contract to pay a definite sum, and the assessment system is a contract to pay pro rata of the proceeds of the assessment. That represents in a nutshell the difference between the two. Now, do you want to know the difference between the two plans of endowment insurance and the old line system? Every contract of endowment insurance can be computed, because it is based on the average life expectation and the compound interest earnings of advance premiums. The assessment endowment plan has no basis on the life expectation nor upon the interest earnings of money, but it is an agreement to pay a certain sum or a proportion of a certain sum of money to old people, at the expense of the young people. It depends for its success upon lapses, and as it holds out inducements not to lapse, it cuts out the very foundation upon which it has any hope of success. I think that about covers the ground.

Q. Do you think that an association that does not publish the full details of the receipts and disbursements in every fund a coöperative association in the true sense of the word? A. I should say not. I should say it was crooked.

Q. As to your experience, do you know whether these endowment associations publish reports and exhibit them, giving details of what they do with the expense fund? A. None of them have ever done so.

Q. What is generally done with the expense fund? A. Well, it is pocketed by the agents and officers; and, moreover, without any exception, they divert a portion of the ordinary receipts or assessments for expenses; in other words, the expenses of these associations are not limited to the dues from fees.

Q. Do not some of them alienate a percentage even of the assessments intended for the reserve fund? A. Yes.

Q. And that reserve fund can be used in case of emergency? A. They take good care that the emergency never arises, for they say, as a rule, that this reserve fund cannot be touched, unless the death rate is in excess of the American table of mortality experience, and that is not likely to ever occur. So that it is a fictitious reserve fund, and a temptation to the cupidity of the managers. It does not add one cent to the security of the insurance.

Q. What class of men are generally engaged in the active work of these organizations? A. Well, they are adventurers; men who live by their wits; men who have failed in every legitimate undertaking.

Q. Are there many insurance men among them? A. Very few.

Q. What class of people are generally taken in by the agents of those concerns? A. The laboring classes—men and women.

Q. Are women to a large extent? A. Women to a large extent. I have received letters from numbers of women who paid out hundreds of dollars and received nothing. As I stated already, I examined the books as an expert. They did not know my business; and I carefully noted that out of one thousand three hundred odd members, over five hundred were women and girls—chambermaids, milliners' assistants, and house servants generally. And of the eight hundred men, a large majority of them were laborers, or belonging to the laboring classes.

Q. A gentleman gave me testimony here two or three days ago, that he was a witness in one of our factories, where a lady canvasser succeeded in getting twelve factory girls into one of these endowment associations? A. It is sheer robbery, as well as practically impossible for them to meet their obligations.

Q. You consider that they are working on an unsound financial basis? A. On an unsound financial basis.

Q. How can you account for the spread of these organizations? A Because it is something like a lottery. If you can account for the success of the lottery it will account for the temporary success of these organizations, because they do distribute prizes in the form of advance loans on the coupons first maturing. That of course advertises them favorably.

Q. Do you favor a law to suppress these bogus endowment associations or to regulate them? A. I would favor a law to bring them under the insurance department, so that they should publish annually, or oftener, a full statement of their receipts and disbursements. I would like to add to the statement I made a moment ago that nearly every northern State with an insurance department has a law requiring all assessment associations

6–L

to make an annual report of their receipts and disbursements. California has not any such law. Now, these endowment associations misuse the term insurance. They are not insurance associations. They don't insure the lives of people. There are only one or two that undertake to pay a coupon to the family of deceased persons, but they don't insure them. It really would be well to suppress that form of insurance entirely, just as Michigan does. This circular means that in Michigan there is no provision in the State laws for assessment endowment insurance.

Q. How, in your opinion, should they be regulated by law? A. They should be suppressed, because it is impossible for them to pay insurance unless they are organized as old line insurance companies, with advance premiums and money placed at compound interest.

Q. Upon what do they profess to depend in order to fulfill their pledges to their members? A. On lapses. They rob Peter to pay Paul.

Q. On new members? A. That is not a very liberal growth, a perpetual growth, which we know is impossible. There must be a limit to that growth in the nature of things, and however honest a man is he inevitably fails. Growth is not essential to the perpetuation of the old line companies.

Q. Do you consider these proprietary companies, such as the Occidental, that you refer to, to be coöperative in any sense? A. Not in any sense.

Q. Do you believe they are sailing under false colors in professing to be coöperative? A. Yes; they certainly are.

Q. Do you believe that the members of these associations have an equal voice with the inside managers in their management? A. No.

Q. And there can be no coöperation unless there is a coöperation of interest and in the management also? A. Yes.

Q. Do you believe that the laws of the State should require inspection of their books and accounts at stated periods by some State officer? A. Yes.

MR. SPELLING: Can you tell any difference, Mr. Bacon, between an assessment and a premium, except in the name? A. Altogether different.

Q. Well, are they not levied and collected just alike? A. Not at all. A man makes a contract of insurance with an organized insurance company; he agrees to pay a premium that is limited and its amount specified. He must pay so much.

Q. Can you tell any actual difference in the privileges and manner of doing business between the regular life insurance companies and those that pay death benefits? Does one enjoy any privileges that are not enjoyed by the other? A. As regards the law?

Q. Yes? A. The old line companies are subject to the law and must make annual reports, and their books are open.

Q. Do the regular insurance companies enjoy any privileges that are not equally enjoyed by any endowment associations in this State that levy assessments? A. No.

Q. Should not the same rights and duties, State supervision, and the requirement to provide a guarantee fund, apply to one as to the other? A. Just as well. That would work no hardship at all to the endowment associations or to the life insurance associations. I imagine that no honest association would object, because the cost of it is nominal.

Q. Was not an effort made at the last meeting of the Legislature to have a bill passed to regulate endowment associations? A. That failed, I am told, on good authority, on account of the opposition of the endowment associations.

Q. If you take a policy of one of these endowment associations that promises to pay, say, $1,000 on a coupon whose maturity is pending when death occurs in consideration of assessments to be levied by the Directors, is not that in effect a life insurance policy? A. That is in effect a policy, not a life insurance policy.

Q. Is it not substantially the same as policies issued by regular companies who comply with the law? A. That I cannot say.

Q. With reference to the force that the Legislature must bring to the present inquiry, do you remember some of the salient features of the bill? A. The salient features of that bill simply required annual reports of receipts and disbursements, and directed the Insurance Commissioner to examine their books at any time.

Q. Mr. Bishop, of the Oakland company, has testified that he had a bill there, or his company was interested in a bill that was introduced into the last Legislature. Do you remember anything of it or know anything about it? A. I don't remember the words of the bill. I know that they had such a bill.

Q. That was a bill in the interests of the endowment associations? A. Yes.

Q. Do you know anything of the bill? A. Well, I don't recollect now.

Q. But you say that legislation was defeated there in consequence of the interposition of members of the endowment associations? A. By the representatives of the endowment companies controlled by officers who came from San Francisco at the call of the companies—so I have been told on good authority.

Q. Have you found, Mr. Bacon, in your experience with these institutions, that it is the ordinary plan of them to change the first plan of assessment where the maturity of the coupon is for a shorter period into one where the maturity is longer? A. I have known of such change in many companies. The new companies have extended their period. They find the plans did not work at first.

Q. Under what section of the law do they claim authority, these endowment associations? A. I think it is Section 451. They claim that they do not do business for profit; they do business for salary and commissions. I don't think that under that law any association has any right to transact business except the purely fraternal; I know that was the design of the law.

COMPLAINTS FROM ENDOWMENT VICTIMS.

STATEMENT OF MARY C. CURRAN, HOLDER OF CERTIFICATE No. 702 IN
THE OCCIDENTAL SELF-ENDOWMENT ASSOCIATION.

STATE OF CALIFORNIA, } ss.
   County of Solano.

Mary Curran first being duly sworn says: I am the mother of Mary C.
Curran, the holder of Certificate No. 702 in the Occidental Self-Endowment
Association; and during all the time the said Mary C. Curran was the
holder thereof, was in daily communication with her.

The said Mary C. Curran is now twenty-four years of age, and is and
has been employed since she was fourteen years of age, continuously, as a
domestic; and thereby earned the money she has paid into the said Occidental Self-Endowment Association.

That the said Mary C. Curran has promptly paid all assessments and
strictly conformed to the by-laws, rules, and regulations of the said association, up to the time of its failure, to wit, March 17, 1889.

That the said Mary C. Curran has paid into the said association as dues
and assessments the amount of —— dollars. That no part thereof has
been returned to her. That all the said sums so paid to said association
herein mentioned were earned by her hard labor.

That the said Mary C. Curran was fully assured that the company was
sound financially, and the representations made to her by the said company's representative, through and by which she was induced to pay the
money aforesaid to said association, and become insured therein, have not
been carried out on the part of the company, and have proven to be false
misrepresentations, and thereby said assured was wrongfully deprived of
her money.

her
MARY X CURRAN.
mark.

Subscribed and sworn to before me this twentieth day of September, A. D.
1889.

CHARLES H. HOBBS.
Notary Public.

I, Mary C. Curran, the assured, have carefully read the foregoing affi-
davit, and it is true.

MARY C. CURRAN.

STATEMENT OF MRS. ELIZABETH WILSON, OF SANTA ROSA, SONOMA COUNTY,
CALIFORNIA.

I was induced to become a certificate holder with the Pacific Mutual
Endowment and Protective Association of Santa Rosa four years ago last
July. I kept my assessments paid up until the Occidental, with which it
consolidated, quit business.

I am a poor woman with a family, and have sat up in bed and sewed when I was not well enough to be out of bed, to earn the money to meet the assessments.

After my assessments were doubled, I went to Judge Overton to ask the reason why they were increased, and he very gruffly replied that he knew nothing about it, that he paid his assessments when due, and then referred me to Mr. Broak for further information.

I then went to Mr. Broak. He explained by saying that in order to meet the maturing coupons, they found it necessary to increase the assessments. I told him how very hard it was for me to make the payments, and asked what shall I do. His reply was, keep them paid up by all means. I considered the Occidental Self-Endowment Association as safe as any bank in the country. I also went to the Directors, and they said the same in substance.

I am now an invalid and a great sufferer, and shall never again be able to bear the duties that devolve upon me, and I make this appeal through the Courts of justice, that my wrongs may be made right inasmuch as I shall receive back the hard earned money I have paid into that association.

MRS. ELIZABETH WILSON.

Subscribed and sworn to before me this twentieth day of September, 1889.

JOHN BROWN,

Justice of the Peace, Santa Rosa township, county and State aforesaid.

STATEMENT OF MRS. ANNIE SECCHITANO, OF SAN JOSÉ.

I am a widow with a large family of children; have a small grocery and fruit store, and depend entirely on the profits of the business for my support.

In May, 1885, I was induced to join the Occidental Self-Endowment Association, then called the Mutual Self-Endowment and Benevolent Association of America, the Pacific Coast department, and took a policy in the same. The promise was held out to me that I should receive loans from time to time, and at the end of four years the sum of $2,000, less the amount loaned to me.

My assessments were very heavy—$20 a month for a greater portion of the time—and it was impossible, with all my self-denial, to meet them from my own income. I was obliged to borrow from various parties, and did borrow on the assurance that I should receive the money from the association as promised. By this means I met and paid all the assessments.

On the failure of the association in March, 1889, I was left with debts incurred for this money borrowed, and am still in debt and using money I need to meet bills for purchases to continue my business, to pay the old debts made to pay assessments.

It has been a great hardship and injury to me.

ANNIE SECCHITANO.

Witness to signature: J. H. LEONARD.

SAN JOSÉ, September 20, 1889.

86

STATEMENT OF MRS. JOSEPH JUGHAM, OF SAN JOSÉ.

I am a widow conducting a small lodging house and doing sewing for my support.

When I joined the Mutual Self-Endowment and Benevolent Association of America, Pacific Coast department, since known as the Occidental Self-Endowment Association, my husband was living, and an invalid unable to work, and I joined, hoping to receive the $1,000 promised me in four years, which would have been October 31, 1889. I was also promised and expected to receive loans from time to time, but never received anything. I met and paid all assessments until the association failed March last, and deprived myself of many comforts to do so. I became doubtful of the stability of the company before it failed, and consulted the Club Manager, R. E. Collins, who told me that he had examined the books, and everything was straight and prosperous, and on this assurance I continued to pay $10 monthly. I need the money which I have paid.

MRS. JOSEPH JUGHAM.

Witness to signature: J. H. LEONARD.

SAN JOSÉ, CAL., September 20, 1889.

STATEMENT OF LOUIS GRIEPENSTRUK, OF SAN JOSÉ.

I, the undersigned, hereby declare that the following statement is true, to wit: That I am a resident of the City of San José, County of Santa Clara, State of California; that I am fifty-three years old; that I have a wife and nine children; that I am a poor man working for a small salary to support my family; that I was induced by the agent of a life insurance company, known as the Occidental Self-Endowment Association, to take a policy for $1,000 in said company; that said agent led me to believe that after twelve months I would receive loans from said company which would be more than sufficient to pay all future assessments, until by the terms and conditions of said policy the first coupon would mature and be paid; that in order to meet these assessments, which in the commencement were payable once in twenty days, but later, by a new resolution or regulation of the managers, once in fifteen days, I was compelled to deprive myself and family of much that was necessary to our comfort; that said company did not meet its obligations, and that I have thereby suffered a pecuniary loss which works a great hardship to myself and family.

LOUIS GRIEPENSTRUK.

Witness to signature: GEORGE KOERBER.

www.ingramcontent.com/pod-product-compliance
Lightning Source LLC
Chambersburg PA
CBHW031447270326
41930CB00007B/896